Calm the
F**k Down

Calm the
F**k Down

How to control what you can
and accept what you can't
so you can stop freaking out
and get on with your life

Sarah Knight

Quercus

First published in 2018 in Great Britain by

Quercus Editions Ltd
Carmelite House
50 Victoria Embankment
London EC4Y 0DZ

An Hachette UK company

A CIP catalogue record for this book is available
from the British Library.

HB ISBN 978 1 78747 619 6
TPB ISBN 978 1 78747 620 2

Illustrations and hand lettering by Lauren Harms

10 9 8 7 6 5 4 3

Printed and bound in Great Britain by Clays Ltd, Elcograf S.p.A.

Contents

CALM THE FUCK DOWN: Identify what you can control, accept what you can't, and let that shit go   67

DEAL WITH IT: Address what you *can* control   155

CHOOSE YOUR OWN ADVENTURE: When shit happens, how will *you* calm the fuck down and deal with it?   **211**

Calm the
F**k Down

A note on the title

This is a book about anxiety — from the white noise of what-ifs to the white-hot terror of a full-blown crisis. As such, you'd be forgiven for thinking I'm the world's biggest asshole for titling it as I have, since everyone knows that the first entry on a long list of Unhelpful Things to Say to a Person Experiencing Anxiety is "Calm the fuck down."

Indeed, when I'm upset and somebody tells me to calm down, I want to murder them in swift and decisive fashion. So I see where you'd be coming from.

But this is also a book about problems — we've all got 'em — and **calming down is exactly what you need to do if you want to *solve* those problems.** It is what it is. So if it keeps you from wanting to murder the messenger, know that in these pages I'm saying "Calm the fuck down" the same way I said "Get your shit together" in the <cough> *New York Times* bestseller of the same name — not to shame or criticize you, but to offer motivation and encouragement.

I promise that's all I'm going for. (And that I'm not the world's biggest asshole; that honor belongs to whoever invented the vuvuzela.)

We cool? Excellent.

One more thing before we dive into all of that anxiety-reducing, problem-solving goodness: **I understand the difference between *anxiety*, the mental illness, and *anxiety*, the temporary state of mind.** I understand it because I myself happen to possess a diagnosis of Generalized Anxiety and Panic Disorder. (Write what you know, folks!)

So although a profanity-riddled self-help book is no substitute for professional medical care, if you picked up *Calm the Fuck Down* because you're perennially, clinically anxious like me, in it you will find plenty of tips, tricks, and techniques to help you manage that shit, which will allow you to **move on to the business of solving the problems that are feeding your anxiety in the first place.**

But maybe you don't have — or don't realize you have, or aren't ready to admit you have — *anxiety,* the mental illness. Maybe you just get temporarily anxious when the situation demands it (see: the white-hot terror of a full-blown crisis). Never fear! *Calm the Fuck Down* **will provide you with ample calamity management tools for stressful times.**

Plus maybe some tips, tricks, and techniques for dealing with that thing you don't realize or aren't ready to admit you have.

Just sayin'.

Introduction

I'd like to kick things off with a few questions:

- How many times a day do you ask yourself *What if?* As in:
  *What if X happens? What if Y goes wrong? What if Z doesn't turn
  out like I want/need/expect it to?*

- How much time do you spend worrying about something
  that hasn't happened yet? Or about something that not
  only hasn't happened, but probably won't?

- And how many hours have you wasted freaking out about
  something that has *already* happened (or avoiding it, as a
  quiet panic infests your soul) instead of just dealing with it?

It's okay to be honest — I'm not trying to shame you. In fact, I'll
go first!

My answer is: *Too many, too much, and a LOT.* I assume yours is too, because if the answer is *Never, none, and ZERO,* then you have no reason to be reading this book (nor, I might add, the hard-won qualifications to have written it).

Well, I come bearing good news.

When we're finished, the next time you come down with a case of the what-ifs — and whether they remain theoretical anxieties or turn into real, live problems that need solvin' — instead of worrying yourself into a panic attack, crying the day away, punching a wall, or avoiding things until they get even worse, you'll have learned to replace the open-ended nature of that unproductive question with one that's much more **logical, realistic, and actionable:**

OKAY, NOW WHAT?

Then, you'll deal with it, whatever it is.

But let's not get ahead of ourselves — for now, we start with the basics.

Shit happens

Boy, does it. And when I think about all the shit that could or probably will happen to me on any given day, I'm reminded of a lyric from departed musical genius and spiritual gangsta, the one, the only, Prince (RIP):

"Dearly Beloved, we are gathered here today to get through this thing called life."

The Purple One had suspect opinions about a lot of things — among them religion, tasteful fabrics, and age-appropriate relationships — but in this regard he was spot-on. Each morning that we wake up and lurch across this rotating time bomb called Earth, our baseline goal is to get through the day. Some of us are angling for more — like success, a bit of relaxation, or a kind word from a loved one. Others are just hoping not to get arrested for treason. (While every day, some of us are hoping someone *else* gets arrested for treason!)

And though each twenty-four-hour cycle brings the potential for good things to happen — your loan gets approved, your girlfriend proposes, your socks match — **there's also the chance that a big steaming pile of shit will land in your lap.** Your house could get repossessed, your girlfriend might break up with you, your socks may become wooly receptacles for cat vomit. Not to mention the potential for earthquakes, tornados, military coups, nuclear accidents, the world wine output falling to record lows, and all manner of disasters that could strike at any time and really fuck up your shit. Especially the wine thing.

That's just how life works. Prince knew it. You know it. And that is literally all you and Prince have in common.

So here's another question for you: **When shit happens, how do you react?** Do you freeze or do you freak out? Do you lock the bathroom door and cry or do you howl at the sky with rage? Personally, I've been known to pretend shit is *not* happening, bury my head in a pillow, and stick my ass in the air in a move I call "ostriching."

Unfortunately, while these coping mechanisms can be comforting, none are especially productive (and I say that having invented one of them). Eventually you have to stop freaking out and start dealing with your shit, and — shocker — **it's hard to make decisions and solve problems when you're panicking or sobbing or shouting, or when all the blood is rushing to your head.**

Which is why what you really need to do, first and foremost, is **calm the fuck down.**

Yes, you.*

---

* If you're having an A-plus day, the sun is shining, the birds are singing, and all is right with your minuscule slice of rotating time bomb, you probably

We've all been there. I simply maintain that most of us could learn how to handle it better. Related: most of us also have a friend, relative, or partner whose inevitable reaction to our every crisis is "Don't worry, everything's going to be okay." Or worse: "Aw, it's not so bad."

On that, I call bullshit. Well-meaning platitudes are easy to offer for someone with no skin in the game. **In this book, we'll be dealing in reality, not nicety.**

The truth is:

Yes, sometimes things will be okay. You pass the test, the tumor comes back benign, Linda returns your text.

But sometimes they won't. Investments go south, friendships fall away, in an election of monumental consequence millions of people cast their vote for an ingrown toenail in a cheap red hat.

In some cases, it's really not so bad, and you *are* overreacting. You've built an imagined crisis up in your head and let it feed your anxiety like a mogwai after dark. If you've seen *Gremlins*, you know how this ends.

But in other cases IT'S REAL BAD BRO, and you? You're *under*reacting. You're like that cartoon dog who sits at a table

---

don't need to calm the fuck down. Congrats. Go outside, enjoy. Things will turn to shit soon enough, and I'll be waiting.

drinking coffee while the house burns down around him thinking *It's fine. This is fine.*

And sure, by saying "everything's going to be okay," your friend/relative/partner is probably just trying to help you. But whether you're making a Taj Mahal out of a teepee, or ignoring a problem for so long that it sets your metaphorical house on fire, I'm *actually* going to help you. That's just how I roll.

Thus begins your education in calming the fuck down:

Lesson #1: Merely *believing* that things will be okay or aren't so bad may make you feel better in the moment, but it won't solve the problem. (And a lot of times it doesn't even feel good in the moment — it feels like you're being condescended to by the Happy Industrial Complex. Don't get me started.)

Either way, it doesn't change a goddamn thing!

Lesson #2: When shit happens, circumstances are what they are: tires are flat, wrists are broken, files are deleted, hamsters are dead. You may be frustrated, anxious, hurt, angry, or sad — but you are right there in the thick of it and the only thing you can control in this equation is YOU, and your reaction.

Lesson #3: To survive and thrive in these moments, you need to ACKNOWLEDGE what's happened, ACCEPT the parts you can't control, and ADDRESS the parts you can.

Per that last one, have you heard of the Serenity Prayer — you know, the one about **accepting the things you cannot change and having the wisdom to know the difference?** *Calm the Fuck Down* is essentially a blasphemous, long-form version of that, with flow-charts 'n' stuff.

If you're into that sort of thing, we're going to get along just fine.

What, me worry?

I'm guessing that if you came to this book for guidance, then worrying about shit — either before or after it happens — is a problem for you. So here's a mini-lesson: **"worrying" has two separate but related meanings.** In addition to the act of anxiously fretting about one's problems, "worrying" also means constantly fiddling with something, rubbing at it, tearing it open, and making it worse.

It's like noticing that your sweater has a dangling thread, maybe the beginnings of a hole. And it's natural to want to pull on it. You're getting a feel for the problem, measuring its potential impact. *How bad is it already? What can I do about it?*

But if you keep pulling — and then tugging, yanking, and fiddling **instead of taking action to fix it** — suddenly you're down a whole sleeve, you're freaking out, and both your state of mind and your sweater are in tatters. I've seen smaller piles of yarn at a cat café.

When you get into this state of mind, you're not just worried *about* something; you're actually *worrying it*. **And in both senses, worrying makes the problem worse.**

This series of unfortunate events applies across the board, **from worries that bring on low-level anxiety to those that precede full-bore freakouts.** Some of that anxiety and freaking out is warranted — like *What if my car runs out of gas in the middle of a dark desert highway?* But some of it isn't — like *What if Linda is mad at me? I know she saw that text I sent yesterday and she hasn't replied. WHY HAVEN'T YOU REPLIED, LINDA???*

Luckily, I'm going to show you how to get a handle on ALL of your worries — **how to accept the ones you can't control, and how to act in a productive way on the ones you can.**

I call it the **NoWorries Method.** It's based on the same concept that anchors all of my work — **"mental decluttering"** — and it has two steps:

Step 1: Calm the fuck down

Step 2: Deal with it

Sounds promising, no?

Or does it sound overly reductive and like it couldn't possibly help you in any way? I hear that, but "overly reductive *yet* extremely helpful" is kind of my thing, so maybe give it another page or two before you decide.

For now, let's circle back to those questions you already admitted you can't stop asking yourself:

What if X happens?
What if Y goes wrong?
What if Z doesn't turn out like I want/need/
expect it to?

The "X" you're worried about could be anything from getting your period on a first date to the untimely death of a loved one. "Y" could be your dissertation defense or the landing gear on your connecting flight to Milwaukee. "Z" might be a job interview, a driving test, or the rather large wager you placed on the latest Royal baby name. (It's a four-thousand-pound shame they didn't go with Gary, I know.)

In the end, it doesn't matter precisely what your what-ifs are — only that they exist and they're occupying some/a lot/too much of your mental space on any given day, unraveling your metaphorical sweater bit by bit. You would therefore do well to note the following:

Lesson #4: A bunch of this shit is unlikely to happen at all.

Lesson #5: You can prevent some of it and mitigate the effects of some of the rest.

Lesson #6: Some of it is and has always been completely out of your hands and locked in the steely grip of Her Majesty, Queen Elizabeth II. You need to take your licks, learn the lesson, and let this one go.

And hey, no judgments. I'm right there with you (hence the hard-won qualifications to have written this book).

For most of my life, I've been a champion worrier. *What-ifs* swirl inside my skull like minnows on a meth bender. I fret about shit that hasn't happened. I obsess over shit that may or may not happen. And when shit does happen, I possess an astounding capacity for freaking out about it.

But over the last few years I've found ways to keep that stuff to a minimum. I'm not completely worry-free, but I have become less anxious and am no longer, shall we say, paralyzed by dread and/or driven to the brink of madness by unmet expectations and a boiling sense of injustice. It's an improvement.

I'm amazed at how good it feels and how much I've been able to accomplish with a relatively simple change in mind-set — **accepting the shit I can't control** — which allows me to focus on dealing with the shit I *can* control, leaving me better equipped to make decisions and solve problems both in the moment and after the fact.

And even to prevent some of them from happening in the first place. Nifty!

I've learned how to stop dwelling on unlikely outcomes in

favor of acting to create more likely ones. How to plow forward rather than agonize backward. And crucially, **how to separate my anxiety about what *might* occur from the act of handling it when it *does* occur.**

You can learn to do all of that too. *Calm the Fuck Down* will help you—

Stop freaking out about shit you can't control.
AND
Enable yourself to make rational decisions.
SO YOU CAN
Solve problems instead of making them worse.

Here's what that process looked like for me during the last few years, and a little taste of how it can work for you.

I can't deal with this shit. (Or can I?)

The beginnings of my change in mind-set happened to coincide with a change of location when my husband and I moved from bustling Brooklyn, New York, to a tranquil fishing village on the north coast of the Dominican Republic.

I know, shut the fuck up, right? But I swear this isn't a story about idyllic, sun-drenched days full of coco locos and aquamarine vistas. I do enjoy those, but the primary benefit of living where I do is that it has forced me — like, aquamarine waterboarded me — to calm down.

During the previous sixteen years in New York, I'd had a lot going on: I climbed the corporate ladder; planned and executed a wedding; bought real estate; and orchestrated the aforementioned move to the Dominican Republic. I was always good at getting shit done, yes, but I was not especially calm while doing it.*

And when anything happened to alter the course of my carefully cultivated expectations — well, *fughetaboutit.*

You might think that a high-functioning, high-achieving, highly organized person would be able to adjust if the situation demanded it. But back then, I couldn't deviate from the plan without experiencing a major freakout — such as when a downpour on the day of my husband's thirtieth-birthday picnic sent me into a fit of *Goodbye, cruel world!*

In those days I had a tendency to melt down faster than a half pound of raclette at a bougie Brooklyn dinner party — **making all of the shit I had to do far more difficult and anxiety-inducing than it needed to be.** Two steps forward, one step back. All. The. Damn. Time.

Something had to give; but I didn't know what, or how to give it.

Which brings us to that tranquil fishing village on the north

---

* Where "not especially calm" equals "a total fucking lunatic."

coast of the Dominican Republic. Three years ago I moved to a place where you might as well abandon planning altogether. Here, the tropical weather shifts faster than the Real Housewives' loyalties; stores close for unspecified periods of time on random days of the week; and the guy who is due to fix the roof *"mañana"* is just as likely to arrive "a week from *mañana*" — possibly because of thunderstorms, or because he couldn't buy the materials he needed from the hardware store that is only periodically and inconsistently open.

Or both. Or neither. Who knows?

Caribbean life may look seductively slow-paced and groovy when you've called in sick from your demanding job to lie on the couch bingeing on chicken soup and HGTV — and in lots of ways it is; I AM NOT COMPLAINING — but it can also be **frustrating for those of us who thrive on reliability and structure, or who don't deal particularly well with the unexpected.**

After a few weeks of hanging out in Hispaniola, I began to realize that if I clung to my old ways in our new life, I would wind up in a perpetual panic about *something*, because *nothing* goes according to plan around here. And THAT would negate the entire purpose of having gotten the hell out of New York in the first place.

So for me, landing in the DR was a shot of exposure therapy with a coconut rum chaser. I've been forced to relax and go with the flow, which has done wonders for my attitude and my Xanax supply.

AGAIN, NOT COMPLAINING.

But through observation and practice, I've also determined that one doesn't need to uproot to an island in the middle of the Atlantic to calm the fuck down.

Anyone can do it — including you.

You just need to shift your mind-set, like I did, to react to problems in a different way. In doing so, you'll also learn that **you actually *can* prepare for the unexpected,** which helps a lot with that whole "one step back" thing.

How is that possible? Wouldn't preparing for every potential outcome drive you crazy in a totally different way?

Well yes, yes it would. But I'm not talking about securing multiple locations for your husband's thirtieth-birthday party because "what if" it rains; or preparing three different versions of a presentation because "what if" the client seems to be in less of a pie chart and more of a bar graph mood that day; or erecting a complicated system of moats around your property because "what if" your neighbor's frisky cows get loose someday. That could definitely drive you crazy in a different way. And possibly to bankruptcy.

I'm talking about **preparing *mentally*.**

That's what this book helps you do, so that when shit happens, you'll have the tools to handle it — **whoever you are, wherever you live, and whenever things get hairy.**

(Pssst: that's what we in the biz call "foreshadowing.")

$$* \quad * \quad *$$

A few months ago after a pleasant night out at a local tiki bar, my husband and I arrived home to an unexpected visitor.

I had opened our gate and was slowly picking my way across the flagstone path to our deck (it was dark, I was tipsy) when a larger-than-usual leaf caught my eye. It seemed to be not so much fluttering on the breeze as...scuttling on it. A quick beam of my iPhone flashlight confirmed that the presumptive almond leaf was in fact a tarantula the size of a honeydew melon.

Yup. I'll give you a moment to recover. Lord knows I needed one.

Now, assuming you haven't thrown the book across the room in disgust (or that you have at least picked it back up), may I continue?

Having previously declared my intention to BURN THE MOTHERFUCKER DOWN if we ever spotted such a creature in our house, I was faced with a quandary. By this time, I had grown fond of my house. And technically, the creature was not *in* it. Just *near* it.

What to do? Stand frozen in place until the thing wandered back to the unknowable depths from whence it came? Sleep with one eye open for eternity? Politely ask the tarantula to skedaddle?

None of those were realistic options. As it turned out, apart from shouting at my husband to "Pleasecomedealwiththetarantula!"

there wasn't much I *could* do. We live in the jungle, baby. And no matter how many real estate agents and fellow expats had told us "those guys stay up in the mountains—you'll never see one," there was no denying the seven-legged fact that one had found its way to our humble sea-level abode.

(You read that correctly. This gent was missing one of his furry little limbs—a fact that will become important later in this story.)

What we *did* do was this: my husband grabbed a broom and used it to guide the uninvited guest off our property and into the neighbors' bushes, and I fled into the house muttering "Everything is a tarantula" under my breath until I was safely upstairs and sufficiently drugged to sleep.

It wasn't totally calming the fuck down, but it was a step in the right direction.

The next morning we got up early to go on an all-day, rum-guzzling boat trip with some friends. (I know, I know, shut the fuck up.) I staggered downstairs in a pre-8:00-a.m. haze and as I turned at the landing toward the bottom of the stairs, I saw it.

Hiding behind the floor-length curtain in the living room was the very same tarantula that had previously been shooed a good hundred feet away from its current position. I knew it was the same one because it had only seven legs. And lest you think I got close enough to count them, I will remind you that *this spider was so fucking big you did not have to get close to it to count its legs*—with which it had, overnight, crossed an expanse of grass, climbed back up onto the deck, and then CLIMBED AGAIN UP TO THE TERRACE AND SQUEEZED IN BETWEEN THE CRACKS OF OUR SLIDING DOORS TO GET INSIDE THE HOUSE.

I know what you're thinking. *THIS is when you burn the mother-fucker down, right?*

And yes, my instinctive reaction was *I can't deal with this shit.*

But you know what? Upon second viewing, the tarantula was not so bad. **Or rather, it was still bad, but *I* was better.**

If we'd found a spider like that inside our Brooklyn apartment, I would have lit a match right then and there. But now it seemed I'd been trained by all those unpredictable monsoon rains and unreliable roof guys: Expect the unexpected! Nothing goes according to plan! *SURPRIIIISE!!!*

From our practice run the night before, I knew it wasn't going to move very fast or, like, start growling at me. And I had to admit that a honeydew-sized spider operating one leg short was a lot smaller and less nimble than a five-foot-tall person with both her legs intact. (It turns out that exposure therapy is clinically sanctioned for a reason.)

By activating the logical part of my brain, I was able to one-up that instinctive *I can't deal with this shit* with a more productive *Okay, well, what are we going to do about this because I have a boat to catch and vast quantities of rum to imbibe.* This was no time for hysterics; **freaking out was not going to solve the problem.**

Recall, if you would, my jacked-up version of the Serenity Prayer:

ACKNOWLEDGE what has happened (a tarantula is in my house)

ACCEPT what you can't control (tarantulas can get into my house?!?)

ADDRESS what you *can* control (get the tarantula out of my house)

I had officially calmed the fuck down — now it was time to deal with it.

Fine, it was time for my husband to deal with it. I helped.

Using an empty plastic pitcher, a broom, a piece of cardboard, and nerves of steel, he trapped the thing humanely and secured it on the dining table while I rounded up sunscreen, towels, portable speakers, and an extra pint of Barceló because last time the boat captain underestimated and really, who wants to hang out on a deserted beach with an infinite supply of coconuts and a finite supply of rum? YOU CAN CONTROL THE RUM.

Then we drove a mile down the road with our new pal Lucky (ensconced in his plastic jug), released the wayward spider into a vacant lot, and boarded the SS *Mama Needs Her Juice*.

* * *

So what do my newfound Caribbean calm and tales of tarantulian derring-do have to do with acknowledging, accepting, and addressing *your* **overactive what-ifs, worries, anxiety, and freakouts?**

A fair question.

In addition to spending many years as a professional worrier, I am currently a professional writer of self-help books, including *The Life-Changing Magic of Not Giving a Fuck, Get Your Shit Together,* and *You Do You.* Each has recounted aspects of my personal trek toward becoming a happier and mentally healthier person, combined with practical, profanity-riddled tips re: accomplishing same.

They call me **"the Anti-Guru."** Not gonna lie, it's a pretty sweet gig.

Collectively, the No Fucks Given Guides — NFGGs, for short — have helped millions of people cast off burdensome obligations, organize their lives, and be their authentic selves. If you are one of those people, I want to thank you for enabling this supersweet gig. If you're new to the party: Welcome! And sorry about the spider stuff. I know that was off-putting, but the NFGGs are like that sometimes. You'll get used to it.

Anyway, I'm glad you're here. And between us, I believe you

are holding in your hands the most useful No Fucks Given Guide of them all, since, as I think we've agreed, everyone has problems.

That's right: You cannot get through life without shit happening to you!

But also: HEREWITH, A MANUAL FOR LEARNING HOW TO COPE!

In *Calm the Fuck Down,* you'll learn about:

- The Four Faces of Freaking Out (and their Flipsides)
- Managing your freakout funds
- Mental decluttering
- The One Question to Rule Them All
- How to sort your problems by probability and prioritize them by urgency
- "Sleight of mind"
- Ostrich Mode and how to avoid it
- Productive Helpful Effective Worrying (PHEW)
- The Three Principles of Dealing With It
- Realistic ideal outcomes (RIOs)
- And much, much more…

So if you're like me — if you've ever thought *I can't deal with this shit*, or if you're asking *What if?* more than you ought to be, worrying too much, freaking out too often, and wasting time and energy obsessing over things you can't control — I can help.

Remember: I'm not here to invalidate or minimize your anxiety or your problems. I just want to assist you in dealing with them, and calming the fuck down is the first step. Along the way, I swear I'll never tell you "everything's going to be okay" or push the narrative that "it's not so bad."

Whatever's going on in your life sucks as hard as you think it does. No arguments here.

But I will say this:

I am 100 percent positive that if I can spend ten minutes in a car with a tarantula on my lap, **you can calm the fuck down and deal with your shit, too.**

1

SO YOU'RE FREAKING OUT:

Acknowledge the real problem and rein in your reaction

In part I, we'll establish some parameters, beginning with what your problems are, exactly, and what variations of havoc they're wreaking on your life.

Could you BE any more excited???

Then we'll study **the evolution of a freakout: how it happens, what it looks like, and what it costs you.** I'll introduce the **Four Faces of Freaking Out and their Flipsides,** and show you how to transition from one to the other. This section includes a primer on a little something known in our household as Mexican Airport Syndrome. Pay attention, amigos.

Next, we'll talk **freakout funds.** These are the resources you have at your disposal to forestall or combat a freakout: **time, energy, and money** — they make the world go round, especially when shit is going down. Plus, there's **the Fourth Fund,** which you may have unknowingly been overdrawing for far too long. We'll discuss.

I'll wrap up part I by explaining the concept of **mental decluttering** (both in general and as it pertains to calming the fuck down); introducing you to **the One Question to Rule Them All;** and finally, walking you through a technique I call **"emotional puppy crating."**

All of this may sound a little wacky (especially the emotional puppy crating), but give it a chance. The way I see it, there are thousands of self-improvement methods on the market that peddle far more suspect solutions to life's problems. At least I know the stuff in this book works, because it works on ME—and in addition to being very logical and rational, I am also, at times, a Bona Fide Basket Case.

Anti-gurus: they're just like us!

Now, let's freak out—together.

What seems to be the problem?

Forgive me for saying so, but you seem a little anxious.

Perhaps it's about something small, like wrapping up the last thing on your to-do list or the niggling concern that you should be calling your parents more often. Maybe you're worried about something bigger or more complicated, like you want to apply to grad school but you're not sure if you can fit it around your day job and budget. The source of your anxiety might be hard to pinpoint, or it could be pretty fucking obvious — like you just totaled your bike, or discovered your house was built on top of an active gopher colony.

Or, and this is just a wild guess, maybe it's all of the above?

Yeah, I kinda thought so.

Well get ready to drop a jaw, because I have news for you: **IT'S ALL CONNECTED.** That low hum of background anxiety, your worries about Shit That Hasn't Happened Yet and Shit That Already Has, the little stuff and the big. All of it is related and **all of it can be attacked with the realism, pragmatism, and logical thinking** that I'll be preaching throughout *Calm the Fuck Down*.

But before you can attack your anxiety *about* it, **you must identify and isolate the specific, underlying problem.** One at a time, please.

Sometimes that's easier said than done. If we're talking about a smashed-up Raleigh or a gopher colony, then I trust you know what's what.* But there may also be days when **you feel *blah* and *blech* for no reason,** and those feelings send you spiraling into the Bad Place.

I can't fall asleep at night.

I woke up in a panic.

I can't relax.

I'm so distracted.

No reason, huh? INCORRECT.

There *is* a reason for your anxiety, a what-if behind your worry. And if you can name it, you'll be in a much better position to calm the fuck down about and deal with it. For example:

I can't fall asleep at night because what if I get bad news from the doctor tomorrow?

I woke up in a panic because what if my presentation goes badly today?

I can't relax because what if I don't study enough to pass the test?

I'm so distracted because what if I forget to do everything I'm supposed to do?

---

* Gopher colonies being a prime example of an underlying problem.

First, you need to figure out *why* you feel this way, so you can figure out *what to do* about it. ACKNOWLEDGE the problem. You do that part, and I'll help with the rest. I think it's a more-than-fair trade for a few minutes of introspection on your part, don't you?

If you woke up in a panic this morning or you're feeling *blah* or *blech* in this very moment, take ten minutes right now to give your tarantulas a name. You don't have to calm down about or deal with them just yet, but get 'em out of the shadows and onto the page.

(If you are not currently experiencing "everything is a tarantula" anxiety, skip this part — but keep it in mind for the future.)

MY TARANTULAS:

_____

_____

_____

_____

Next up, I'll show you **what happens when your worries and what-ifs leave you not merely distracted or unable to sleep, but barreling toward a full-fledged freakout.**

Why am I taking you deep into the Bad Place? Because understanding how freaking out works will help you understand how to *avoid it.*

The evolution of a freakout

Imagine you're hosting your daughter's high school graduation party this weekend. She's headed off to the University of Texas; you're very proud. And although you tallied the RSVPs thrice and calculated your provisions accordingly, what if more people show up than you expected?

You start to worry that you don't have enough food and drink to serve all of your guests, plus the inevitable plus-ones, *plus* a half dozen teenage boys who will undoubtedly show up unannounced and decimate the hot dog supplies, leaving you with a subpar grilled-meat-to-potato-salad ratio far too early in the day.

This is normal. Show me someone who's planned a big event and hasn't been plagued by what-ifs and worries and I'll show you a superhuman who runs on Klonopin and hubris.

It's what you do (or don't do) next that counts.

You could run out and grab an extra pack of dogs, and just throw them in the freezer if they don't get eaten. By taking action — tying a knot in that loose thread — you can prevent this worry from destroying your metaphorical sweater.

Or, instead of acknowledging the problem (potential meat shortage), accepting what you can't control (uninvited guests), and addressing what you can (dog quantities), you could just keep worrying.

Let's say you do that.

What if the citronella torches don't keep the mosquitos away as advertised? What if it rains? What if the UT novelty coasters I ordered don't get here in time?

Uh-oh. Your sweater is unraveling knit one by purl two — and those are just the logistical what-ifs! You can't help yourself. You keep pulling and tugging and adding more to the mix:

What if people take one look at my yard decorations and think I'm trying too hard? (Or not hard enough?) What if the neighbors are annoyed by all the cars parked along the street? What if we did all this work and everybody cancels at the last minute?

Now your sweater is more of a midriff top, you can't stop to breathe, let alone take action, and you're no longer merely worried — you're officially freaking out.

EVOLUTION OF A FREAKOUT:

WHAT-IF
↓
WORRY
↓
INACTION
↓
FREAKOUT!

This is how it happens. And with the proper training, you should be able to prevent it.

In part II, for example, we'll practice **identifying what you can control** (investing in a few cans of industrial-strength bug spray, a tent, and expedited shipping) **and accepting what you can't** (next-door neighbor Debbie's disdain for orange-and-white floral arrangements; everyone you invited gets chicken pox) **so you can prepare for some outcomes and let go of your worries about others.** Go Longhorns!

But for the moment, and for the sake of a good ol' cautionary tale, let's stick to diagnostics. **Because whether it's bubbling up or already boiling over, it helps to know which *type* of freakout you're experiencing.**

They all look different and there are different ways to defuse each of them.

The Four Faces of Freaking Out

In my previous books, I've been known to offer a neat taxonomy of the different types of readers who could benefit from taking my advice. I do this because I find that encountering a somewhat personalized profile helps one feel seen, which is comforting when one is about to be smacked upside the head with some decidedly uncomfortable truths.

Which makes it unfortunate for you and me both that **Freak-**

ing Out, How Everybody Does It and Why, is all over the god-damn map.

Some of us don't blink an eye when our septic tanks back up, but hyperventilate if Starbucks runs out of almond croissants. Others pull a Cool Hand Luke when the car gets towed or the test results come back positive, but reach our own personal DEFCON 1 when the cable goes out during *America's Next Top Model*.

Furthermore, **freaking out manifests in different strokes for different folks.** For some it's the openmouthed, panic-sweating countenance of a *Cathy* cartoon from the eighties ("Ack!"); but for others, freaking out is more about tears than tremors. Or black moods. Or blank stares.

And to top it all off — any one of us might experience a different form of freakout on a different day, for a different reason.

For example, *you* may not be a big dumb crybaby like your friend Ted who spends all day posting "feeling emotional" emoji on Facebook, but if you lose your wedding ring or your grandma, you're liable to get a little weepy. And *I* don't typically waste my breath screaming and shouting, but one time in 2001 I opened the refrigerator door on my foot and the resulting spittle-filled tirade was not unlike Jack Nicholson's turn on the stand in *A Few Good Men*.

As I said, all over the map.

So instead of trying to fit you, as an individual freaker-outer, into one tidy category, I've winnowed the types of freakouts themselves into four big, messy categories — any one or more of which you might fall into at any given time:

Anxiety

Sadness

Anger

Avoidance (aka "Ostrich Mode")

These are the Four Faces of Freaking Out — the masks we wear when we worry obsessively — and *ooh, mama* it's getting hard to breathe up in this piece. Your job is to learn how to recognize them, so you can fight back.

Know your enemy and all that.

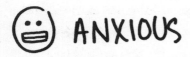 ANXIOUS

What it looks like: Anxiety comes in many forms, and for the uninitiated it can sometimes be hard to label. For example, you may think you've got a touch of food poisoning, when your upset stomach is actually due to anxiety. Or you might think you've *been poisoned* when really you're just having an old-fashioned panic attack. (Been there, thought that.) Other indicators include but are not limited to: nervousness, headaches, hot flashes, shortness of breath, light-headedness, insomnia, indecision, the runs, and compulsively checking your email to see if your editor has responded to those pages you sent an hour ago.

(And remember, you don't have to be diagnosed with capital-A Anxiety Disorder to experience lowercase-a anxiety. Plenty of calm, rational, almost-always-anxiety-free people go through occasional bouts of situational anxiety. Good times.)

Why it's bad: Apart from the symptoms I listed above, one of the most toxic and insidious side effects of being anxious is **OVER-THINKING.** It's like that buzzy black housefly that keeps dipping and swooping in and out of your line of vision, and every time you think you've drawn a bead on it, it changes direction. Up in the corner! No, wait! Over there by the stairs! Uh-oh, too slow! Now it's hovering three feet above your head, vibrating like the physical manifestation of your brain about to explode. WHERE DO YOU WANT TO BE, HOUSEFLY??? MAKE UP YOUR MIND.

Overthinking is the antithesis of productivity. I mean, have you ever seen a fly land anywhere for more than three seconds? How much could they possibly be getting accomplished in any given day?

What can you do about it? You need to Miyagi that shit. Focus. One problem at a time, one *part* of that problem at a time. And most important: one *solution* to that problem at a time. Lucky for you, part II contains many practical tips for accomplishing just that.

Keep reading, is what I'm saying.

 SAD

What it looks like: Weeping, moping, rumpled clothes, running mascara, the scent of despair, and heaving breathless heaving breaths. It can also lead to a condition I call Social Media Self-Pity, which is tiring not only for you, but also for your friends and followers. Cut it out, Ted. Nobody wants to watch you have an emotional breakdown in *Garfield* memes.

Why it's bad: Listen, I've got absolutely nothing against a good cry. You're worried that your childhood home is going to be bull-dozed by evil city planners or that your hamster, Ping-Pong, might not make it out of surgery? By all means, bawl it out. I do it all the time. Catharsis!

Just try not to, you know, *wallow*.

When worrying becomes wallowing—letting sadness over-take you for long periods of time—you've got bigger problems. Ongoing sadness is **EXHAUSTING**. As energy flags, you might stop eating or leaving the house, which compounds the encroach-ing lethargy. You'll get less and less productive. And all of *that* can lead to feeling depressed and giving up on dealing with your shit altogether.

But to be clear, being sad — even for a messy, depressing stretch — is one thing. Having clinical depression is another. If you think you might not be merely sad, but fully in the grip of depression, I urge you to seek help beyond the pages of a twenty-dollar book written by a woman whose literal job is to come up with new ways to work "fuck" into a sentence.

Though if that woman may be so bold: depression, like anxiety, can be hard to suss out when you're the detective and your own head is the case. Do yourself a favor and listen to people around you when they say "Hey, you seem not merely sad, but fully in the grip of depression. Maybe you should talk to a professional?" And don't be ashamed about it. All kinds of people — even ones with objectively hunky-dory lives — can suffer from depression. Mental illness is a bitch.*

All of this is to say, I may not be qualified to diagnose or treat you for depression (the disease); but under the auspices of *Calm the Fuck Down,* I think feeling depressed (the state of mind) is fair game. And to my mind, that state is *exhausted.*

What can you do about it? Patience, my pretties. We're gonna get you up and out of bed sooner rather than later. It's what Ping-Pong would have wanted.

---

* Welp, looks like I found a title for my next book!

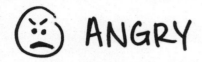 # ANGRY

What it looks like: Painful encounters with fridge doors not-withstanding, I don't tend to get angry. Maybe it's because my parents didn't fight in front of me. Maybe it's just my natural temperament. Or maybe it's because I'm a stone-cold bitch who skips getting mad and goes straight to getting even. But even though I don't do a lot of yelling, screaming, wishing poxes on people, or setting fire to their prized possessions myself, that doesn't mean I don't know the drill. Those in the throes of anger experience unhealthy side effects such as rising blood pressure and body temperature, the desire to inflict physical violence and the injuries sustained upon doing so, splotchy faces, clenched jaws, and unsightly bulging neck tendons.

But an invisible — though no less damaging — result of an angry freakout is that it impedes good judgment. **IT MAKES THINGS WORSE.**

Why it's bad: In the age of smartphone cameras, every meltdown is a potential fifteen minutes of infamy. Do you want to wind up on the evening news spewing regrettable epithets or on Facebook Live destroying public property because you couldn't calm the fuck down? No, you do not. Behold: Mexican Airport Syndrome.

Mexican Airport Syndrome

Once upon a time my husband and I were returning from a family vacation that had been organized by a travel agent. Somehow, when the thirteen of us got to our connecting flight in Mexico City, I didn't have a ticket. Not a seat assignment, mind you, but *a fucking ticket*. Who knows what had happened, but you know what doesn't fix it? Getting all up in the face of the airline employee manning the check-in desk. My [sweet, generous, kind, typically very calm] husband nearly learned this lesson the hard way when he lost his shit on one of said employees for about three-point-two seconds before I elbowed him in the ribs and communicated *I don't want to get detained overnight — or forever — in Mexico City* with my eyes. Also saving his *tocineta* that day was the Long Island mom who was having the same problem and dealing with it in an exponentially worse way. Do you know that she has a Very Important Bar Mitzvah to attend tomorrow?!? Right. I got on the plane. She didn't.

What can you do about it? Well, you could take an anger management class, but that doesn't sound very pleasant. I have a few stimulating alternatives I think you're going to like. (Especially page 115. That's a good one.)

PS If I'm being honest, I'm curious about what it'll take to activate my Anger face. It's been a good fifteen years since the Refrigerator Incident and ya girl is only human.

 # AVOIDANCE
(aka Ostrich Mode)

What it looks like: The tricky thing about Ostrich Mode is that you may not even realize you're doing it, because "doing it" is quite literally "doing nothing." You're just ignoring or dismissing warnings and pretending like shit isn't happening. Nothing to see here, folks! Head firmly in the sand.

(BTW, I know these giant birds do not really bury their disproportionately tiny heads in the sand to escape predators, but I need you to lighten up a little when it comes to the accuracy of my metaphors; otherwise this book will be no fun for either of us.)

Now, sometimes the 'strich stands alone — if you're merely putting off a mundane chore, that's pure, unadulterated avoidance. Other times, ostriching is the result of having *already* succumbed to anxiety, sadness, and/or anger. In those moments it feels like your brain is a pot of boiling lobsters, and if you can just keep the lid tamped down tightly enough, maybe you'll never have to confront their silent screams. (This is typically when I dive headfirst for the couch pillows.)

Why it's bad: First of all, un-dealt-with shit begets *more shit.* Ignoring a jury summons can lead to fines, a bench warrant, and a misdemeanor on your permanent record. Pretending like you haven't developed late-life lactose intolerance can lead to embarrassing dinner party fallout. And refusing to tend to that pesky wound you got while chopping down your Christmas tree may mean spending the New Year learning to operate a prosthetic hand better than you operate an axe.

And second, while I concede that willfully ignoring whatever shit may be happening to you is a shrewd means of getting around having to acknowledge, accept, or address it — guess what? If your worries have sent you into Ostrich Mode, you haven't actually escaped them. They'll be sitting right outside your hidey-hole the next time you lift your head. (Hi, guys. Touché.) Avoidance means **NEVER, EVER SOLVING YOUR PROBLEM.**

What can you do about it? Great question. Just by asking, you're already making progress.

Survey says: y'all are a bunch of freaks

As part of my research for *Calm the Fuck Down,* I conducted an anonymous online survey asking people to name their go-to freakout reaction. It revealed that most folks (38.6 percent) fall into the "Anxious/Panicky" category; 10.8 percent each cop to "I get angry" and "I avoid things"; and another 8.3 percent pledge allegiance to "Sad/Depressed." As for the rest? Nearly one third of respondents (30.3 percent) said "I can't pick just one. I do all of these things," which was when I knew this book would be a hit. And a mere 1.2 percent said "I never do any of these things." Sure you don't.

Welcome to the Flipside

Okay, I was saving the nitty-gritty practical stuff for part II, but you've been so patient with all these parameters that I want to give you a sneak peek at **how we're going to flip the script** on whichever Freakout Face you're experiencing.

I've based my method on a little gem called Newton's Third Law of Motion, which states that **"for every action, there is an equal and opposite reaction."**

You don't have to have taken high school physics (which I didn't, as may be obvious from my forthcoming interpretation of this law) to understand the idea that you can counteract a bad thing with a good thing. Laughing is the opposite of crying. Deep breaths are the opposite of lung-emptying screams. The pendulum swings both ways, et cetera, et cetera.

Ergo, one simple route to calming down pre-, mid-, or post-freakout is to — cue Gloria Estefan — **turn the beat around.**

FREAKOUT FACES: THE FLIPSIDES

Anxious and overthinking?	**FOCUS:** Which of these worries takes priority? Which can you actually control? Zero in on those and set the others aside. (A bit of a recurring theme throughout the book.)

Sad and exhausted?	**REPAIR WITH SELF-CARE:** Treat yourself the way you would treat a sad friend in need. Be kind. Naps, chocolate, baths, cocktails, a *South Park* marathon; whatever relieves your funk or puts a spring back in your step and a giggle in your wiggle.
Angry and making shit worse?	**PEACE OUT WITH PERSPECTIVE:** You can't elbow yourself in the ribs like I did to my husband in the Mexico City airport (seriously, elbows don't bend in that direction). But when you're getting hot under the collar, you can *imagine* what it would be like to live out your days in a south-of-the-border airport holding pen. Visualize the consequences and adjust your attitude accordingly.
Avoiding and prolonging the agony?	**ACT UP:** Take one step, no matter how small, toward acknowledging your problem. Say it out loud. Write it in steam on the bathroom mirror. Fashion its likeness into a voodoo doll. If you can do that, you're on your way to calming the fuck down.

So there you have it: **a simple framework for acknowledging your worries, recognizing your unhealthy reactions, and beginning to reverse them.**

I mean, I didn't become an internationally bestselling anti-guru by making this shit *hard* for you guys.

Freakout funds

In *The Life-Changing Magic of Not Giving a Fuck* I introduced the concept of "fuck bucks," which are the resources — **time, energy, and money** — that you spend on everything you care about, from activities and appointments to friends, family, and more. Conversely, you can choose to *not* spend those resources on things you *don't* care about. Managing them is called "making a Fuck Budget," a concept that is on track to become my most enduring legacy. A *Lemonade* for anti-gurus, if you will.

Since you don't fix what ain't broke, I carried fuck bucks and the budgeting thereof through the next book, *Get Your Shit Together* — the premise being that you also have to spend time, energy, and/or money on things you MUST do, even if you don't really WANT to do them — like, say, going to work so you can earn money so you can pay your rent. In the epilogue, I warned (presciently, as it turns out) that **"shit happens"** and **"you might want to reserve a little time, energy, and money for that scenario, just in case."**

Thus, in *Calm the Fuck Down* — because I am nothing if not a maker-upper of catchy names for commonsense concepts that we should all be employing even if we didn't have catchy names for them — I give you **freakout funds (FFs)**.

These are the fuck bucks you access when shit happens. You could spend them exacerbating all the delightful behavior I went over in the previous section. **Or you could spend them calming the fuck down and dealing with the shit that caused said freakout.**

Ideally, you've read *Get Your Shit Together* and saved up for this scenario. If not, you're in even more need of the following tutorial. But any way you slice it, their quantities are limited and **every freakout fund spent is time, energy, or money deducted from your day.**

TIME

Time has been in finite supply since, well, since the beginning. They're not making any more of it. Which means that eventually you're going to run out of time to spend doing everything — including freaking out about or dealing with whatever is about to happen/is happening/just happened to you. Why waste it on the former when spending it on the latter would vastly improve the quality of your entire remaining supply of minutes?

ENERGY

You will also eventually run out of energy, because although Jeff Bezos is trying really hard, he has not yet programmed Alexa to suck out your mortal soul while you're sleeping and recharge you on Wi-Fi. At some point, you have to eat, rest, and renew the old-fashioned way — and if the shit does hit the fan, you'll wish you'd spent less energy freaking out about it and had more left in the tank to devote to dealing with it.

MONEY

This one's more complex, since some people have a lot and some people have none, and everyone's ability to replenish their coffers varies. But if you're broke, then stress-shopping while you freak out about passing the bar exam is obviously poor form. Whereas if you've got a bottomless bank account, you might argue that cleaning out the J.Crew clearance rack is at least contributing to the improvement of your overall mood. I'm not one to pooh-pooh anyone's version of self-care, but all that money you spent on khaki short-shorts and wicker belts is definitely not *solving the underlying problem* of your LSAT scores. Hiring a tutor would probably be a better use of funds. (And to all my billionaire doomsday preppers out there with money to burn: you do you, but I have a hunch neither your guns nor your bitcoin will be worth shit on the Zombie Exchange.)

In sum: **Worrying is wasteful.** It costs you time, energy, and/or money and gives you nothing useful in return. Whereas if you spend your freakout funds actually dealing with something, you've, you know — actually dealt with it.

My goal is to help you minimize your worrying and spend your FFs wisely along the way.

Nice try, Knight. If I could stop worrying and retain a viselike grip over my time, energy, and money, I'd BE Jeff Bezos by now.

Hey, calm the fuck down — I said "minimize." I personally hold the Women's World Record for Worrying Every Day About Dying of Cancer. Nobody's perfect. **But when you find yourself worrying to the point of freaking out, you should consider the resources you're wasting on that futile pursuit.**

Anxious? Overthinking is overspending.

Sad? After you've spent all that energy on crying, wailing, beating your chest, and feeding the depressive beast, you've got nothing left with which to deal.

Angry? This might be the biggest misuse of freakout funds, since it usually *adds* to your debt. Like when you get so mad at the amount of time you've

---

3 ways in which overthinking wastes time, energy, and money

If you change your outfit seven times before you go out, you'll be late.

If you spend more time fiddling with fonts than writing your term paper, you'll never turn it in.

If you keep second-guessing him, your interior decorator will fire you and you'll lose your deposit.

spent on hold with Home Depot Customer Service that you throw your iPhone at the wall, crack the screen, dent the Sheetrock, and drop the call—which means you haven't solved your original problem (faulty birdbath), AND you've added two new line items to your real and metaphorical bills.

Ostriching? Don't think you guys are getting away with anything. Even by avoiding your shit, you're depleting your FFs. You've wasted a lot of valuable time—a nonrenewable resource that could have been put toward solutions—doing a whole lot of nothing. You've also wasted energy contorting yourself into pretending *EVERYTHINGISFINEJUSTFINE*.

Remember that cartoon dog? He's a pile of cartoon embers now.

No matter which type of freakout you're experiencing or trying to avoid, **there are wiser ways to deploy your funds.** For example:

- Instead of wasting TIME worrying about failing your physics class, you could spend it mocking up some quantum flash cards.

- Instead of wasting ENERGY pacing around the apartment worrying about what's going to happen when your roommate gets home and sees that the dog, Meatball, has had his way with someone's favorite Air Jordans, you could spend that energy researching obedience schools for Meatball.

- And instead of spending MONEY on quacky products that will supposedly prevent you from going bald but don't actually work, you could buy yourself a few really cool hats and become Really Cool Hat Guy.

Welcome to the Flipside, stranger. Fancy meeting you here.

(In other news, I'm pretty sure at least three readers and one dog have already gotten their money's worth out of this book.)

The Fourth Fund

Curtis "50 Cent" Jackson had *The 50th Law*. I have the Fourth Fund, an offshoot of fuck bucks that I developed exclusively for *Calm the Fuck Down*. This is HOT HOT ORIGINAL CONTENT right here, folks.

We all have that friend or family member or coworker or fellow volunteer at the food co-op who seems to be in **Constant Crisis Mode,** don't we? I'll call her Sherry. There isn't a date that hasn't stood Sherry up, an asshole that hasn't rear-ended her in the parking lot, a deadline that hasn't been COMPLETELY BLOWN by one of her clients, or a bucket of compost that hasn't been upended on her lap by a careless stoner wearing those godawful TOMS shoes that make your feet look like mummified remains.

You want to be sympathetic when Sherry kvetches about her latest catastrophe or shows up to the morning meeting all sweaty and blinking rapidly and going on and on about *Would you believe the shit I have to deal with?!*

But the thing is, she does this all the time. So you also kind of want to be like, *What's your problem* now, *you freakshow? Just calm the fuck down and deal with it. Jesus.* (If you can't relate to this sentiment at all, you're a better person than I am. Enjoy your priority seating in the Afterlife.)

This brings us to the **Fourth Fund: Goodwill.**

GOODWILL

Unlike time, energy, and money, the goodwill account is not held by you. It is funded by the sympathy and/or assistance of *others*, and is theirs to dole out or withhold as they see fit. Your job is to keep your account in good standing by not being a fucking freakshow all the time like Sherry.

What Sherry doesn't realize is **how much sympathy she erodes when she brings her constant crises to your front door.** At some point you'll start shutting it in her face like you do with Jehovah's Witnesses or little kids looking for their ball.

What? They shouldn't have kicked it in my yard. It's my ball now.

Anyway, now let's turn the tables and say *you're* the one looking for sympathy from your fellow man. That's cool. It's human nature to commiserate. Like making conversation about the weather, we all do it—we bitch, we moan, we casually remark on how warm it's gotten lately as though we don't know a ninety-degree summer in Ireland foretells the death of our planet.

When you're feeling overcome by the sheer magnitude of your personal misfortune, it's understandable to cast about for and feel buoyed by the sympathy of others.

Sometimes you just want a friend to agree with you that you shouldn't have had to wait around forty-five minutes for the cable guy to show up and then realize he didn't have the part he needed to connect your box, causing you to get so mad that you broke a tooth chomping down in frustration on the complimentary pen he left behind. What good is a fucking *pen* going to do you when all you want is to be able to watch Bravo and now you have to go to the fucking *dentist,* which is undoubtedly going to ruin another entire day! Or maybe you just need to let someone—anyone—know that Jeremy the Assistant Marketing VP is the absolute, goddamn *worst!*

I hear ya. (So does everybody in a fifty-foot radius. You might want to tone it down just a touch.) And when your friends, family, and fellow volunteers see you in distress, their first reaction will probably be to sympathize with you. They wouldn't be working at a food co-op if they weren't bleeding-heart socialists.

But this is where the Fourth Fund comes into play: **if you freak out *all* the time, about *everything,* you're spending heavily against your account of goodwill.** You're in danger of overdrawing it faster than they drain the aquarium after a kid falls into the shark tank, resulting in the classic Boy Who Cried Shark conundrum:

When you need the help and sympathy for something worthy, it may no longer be there.

<hums *Jaws* theme song>

<sees self out>

Hot take, coming right up!

If you'll indulge me in a brief tangent, I have some real talk for my fellow Anxiety-with-a-capital-A sufferers who find themselves in Constant Crisis Mode more often than not.

Due to my then-undiagnosed Generalized Anxiety Disorder, I spent years treating my friends, family, colleagues, and husband to all of my mysterious stomachaches and last-minute cancellations and office crying and whirling-dervish-like propensity for reorganizing other people's homes without permission.

Most of them couldn't understand why I was freaking out all

the time. To them, the majority of my worries didn't seem worthy of such chaos and insanity.

What's your problem now, you freakshow? Just calm the fuck down and deal with it. Jesus.

Sound familiar?

Some of these peeps began to withdraw, withholding their sympathy and support — and they weren't always able to hide their annoyance or frustration with me, either. At the time, I was confused. A little bit hurt. Righteously indignant, even. But today, with the benefit of both hindsight and therapeutic intervention, you know what?

I DON'T BLAME THEM. It's not the rest of the world's job to deal with my shit.

Harsh? Maybe, but I get paid to tell it like it is.

As I've said, I know exactly how badly *anxiety,* the mental illness, can fuck with us — and it's awesome when our family and friends can learn about it and help us through it. I'm eternally grateful to my husband for putting up with a few years of extreme unpleasantness before beginning to understand and accept my anxiety. It's still unpleasant sometimes, but at least he knows that **now *I* know what the underlying problem is,** and that I'm trying to keep it in check — which deposits a lot more goodwill into my account than when I spent most of my time sleeping and crying and not doing anything to change my situation.

So if I may make a potentially controversial argument:

Some of us get dealt worse hands than others, and deserve a little overdraft protection, but the Bank of Goodwill shouldn't extend lifetime credit just because *you* have some issues to work through.

If not a day goes by when you don't don your Anxious Freakout Face — and consequently get all up in other people's faces with your problems — then it may be time to consider that You. Are. Part. Of. Your. Problem.

Am I a monster? I don't think so. A blunt-ass bitch maybe, but you already knew that. And this blunt-ass bitch thinks that **we actually-clinically-anxious people need to take some personal responsibility.** We need to acknowledge our tendencies, do some soul-searching, and maybe go to a doctor or therapist or Reiki healer or something and sort out our shit, **lest we risk alienating our entire support system.**

To put it another way: If you had chronic diarrhea, you'd be looking into ways to stop having chronic diarrhea, right? And what if it was affecting your relationships because you couldn't go to parties or you were always canceling dates at the last minute or when you *were* at other people's houses you were so distracted by your own shit (literally) that you weren't being very good company anyway? You wouldn't want to continue shitting all over your friends (figuratively), would you?

I thought so. Moving on.

Mental decluttering and the One Question to Rule Them All

We're getting down to the last of the brass tacks here in part I. We've gone over **the importance of naming your problems, understanding your reaction to those problems, and valuing your response.** It's time to segue into *how,* exactly, you're supposed to put all of those lessons into action and begin calming the fuck down.

Enter: **mental decluttering.**

If you've read any of the NFGGs or watched my TEDx Talk, you're familiar with the concept; I'll try to explain it succinctly enough to first-timers that it won't send the rest of you flocking to Amazon to complain that "Knight repeats herself."*

Here's how it works:

Just like the physical decluttering made popular in recent years by Japanese tidying expert and author of *The Life-Changing Magic of Tidying Up* Marie Kondo, **mental decluttering** (made popular by anti-guru, sometime parodist, and author of *The Life-Changing Magic of Not Giving a Fuck* Sarah Knight) has two steps:

DISCARDING and ORGANIZING

---

* It's a series, guys. Cut a bitch some slack.

The difference is, my version of discarding and organizing happens entirely in your mind, not in your drawers or closets or garage.

There is no physical exertion involved. You won't catch me chanting, ohm-ing, or downward dogging my way through this shit. You're free to engage in those activities if you wish, whether it's to calm the fuck down or just to pick up nice single moms named Beth at the YMCA. But it's not required.

(Will mental decluttering eventually leave you feeling physically refreshed? It sure will! After all, fewer panic attacks and rage-gasms are good for your heart, your lungs, and the tiny bones in your feet that tend to break when you kick things that are not meant to be kicked. But that's not the primary focus, just a snazzy by-product.)

The two steps of mental decluttering align not at all coincidentally with the two steps of the NoWorries Method.

Step 1: DISCARD your worries (aka calm the fuck down)

Step 2: ORGANIZE your response to what's left (aka deal with it)

That's it. Discard, then organize. And the way you begin is by looking at whatever problem you're worried about and asking yourself a very simple question.

> ### The One Question to Rule Them All
>
> Can I control it?
>
> This inquiry informs every shred of advice I'll be giving for the remainder of the book. Just like Marie Kondo asks you to decide if a material possession brings joy before you discard it, or like I ask you to decide if something annoys you before you stop giving a fuck about it, asking "Can I control it?" is the standard by which you'll measure whether something is worth your worries — and what, if anything, you can do about it.

Mental decluttering and the One Question to Rule Them All really shine in part II, but before we get there, I have one last parameter I want to parametate, which is this:

When what-ifs become worries and worries become freakouts and freakouts make everything harder and more miserable than it ever had to be, **one of the things you can control right away is your *emotional response.***

With that, I'll turn it over to man's best friend…who is also sometimes man's worst enemy.

(Please don't tell John Wick I said that.)

This is your brain on puppies

Emotions are like puppies. Sometimes they're purely fun and diverting; sometimes they're comforting or distracting; sometimes they just peed on your mother-in-law's carpet and aren't allowed in the house anymore.

In any case, **puppies are good for short periods of time until you have to get something accomplished,** and then you need to coax them into a nice, comfy crate because you cannot — I repeat: CANNOT — deal with your shit while those little fuckers are on the loose.*

It doesn't even matter if these are "bad" puppies/emotions or "good" puppies/emotions. (Emuppies? Pupmotions?) ALL puppies/emotions are distracting. It's in their nature. You can totally get derailed by positive emotions — like if you're so excited that the Oreo McFlurry is back, you go straight to the drive-through having forgotten that it was your turn to pick up your kid at preschool. Oops.

But I think we both know that happy and excited to make digestive love to diabetes in a cup aren't the emotions *Calm the Fuck Down* is here to help you corral.

What we're trying to do is take the freakout-inducing puppies/emotions and:

Grant them a reasonable visitation period in which to healthily acknowledge their existence;

---

* Please don't email me about the detriments of crate-training your dog. Please. I'm sitting up and begging you.

Give them a chance to wear themselves out with a short burst of activity;

And then exile them while we get to work on solving the problems that brought them out to play in the first place.

Quick reminder

Hi, it's me, not a doctor or psychologist! Nor am I a behavioral therapist! Honestly, I can't even be trusted to drink eight glasses of water every day and I consider Doritos a mental health food. But what I do have is the learned ability to relegate emotions to the sidelines as needed, so that I can focus on logical solutions. This is my thing; it's what works for me and it's why I have written four No Fucks Given Guides and not the *Let's All Talk About Our Feelings Almanac*. If you *do* happen to be a doctor, psychologist, or therapist and you don't approve of sidelining one's emotions in order to calm the fuck down and deal with one's shit, first of all, thanks for reading. I appreciate the work you do, I respect your game, and I hope my Olympic-level floor routine of caveats makes it clear that I'm presenting well-intentioned, empirically proven suggestions, not medical fact. If you could take this into consideration before clicking that one-star button, I would greatly appreciate it.

Alright, just to be sure we're all on the same emotionally healthy page, let me be superduper clear:

- **It's okay to have emotions.** Or as another guru might put it: "*You've* got emotions! And *you've* got emotions! And *you've* got emotions!" Having them is not the problem; it's when you let emotions run rampant *at the expense of taking action* that you start having problems (see: The evolution of a freakout).

- **In fact, there's a lot of science that says you must allow yourself to "feel the feels" about the bad stuff — that you have to go *through* it to get *past* it.** This is especially true when it comes to trauma, and I'm not advising you to ignore those problems/emotions. Just to sequester them periodically like you would an unruly puppy. (See: I am not a doctor.)

- **It's even okay to freak out a little bit.** To yell and scream and ostrich every once in a while. We're not aiming for "vacant-eyed emotionless husk." That's some prelude-to-going-on-a-killing-spree shit, right there, and not an outcome I wish to promote to my readership.

That said — and in my decidedly nonscientific opinion — when your emuppies are running amok, it's time to lock 'em up and at least temporarily misplace the key. What I will henceforth refer to as **emotional puppy crating** has been useful to me in the following scenarios:

It's how I continued to enjoy my wedding reception after the train of my dress caught on fire, instead of going on a champagne rampage against the culprit. Love you, Mom!

It's how I managed to write and deliver a eulogy for my uncle's funeral instead of being incapacitated by grief.

It's how we decided to call an emergency plumbing hotline at 2:00 a.m. when the upstairs neighbor's toilet went Niagara Falls into our bathroom, instead of succumbing to despair (and sleep) and making everything that much worse (and wet) for ourselves the next day.

First, I acknowledge the emotion — be it anxiety, anger, sadness, or one of their many tributaries (e.g., fear) — and then I sort of mentally pick it up by the scruff of the neck and quarantine it in a different part of my brain than the part that I need to use to deal with the problem at hand. **If you practice mindfulness, you might know this trick as "Teflon mind," so termed because negative thoughts aren't allowed to stick.** I think the puppy analogy is more inviting than the image of an eight-inch frying pan anywhere near my skull, but tomato, tomahto.

Am I successful every time? Of course not! In addition to being not a doctor, I am also not an all-powerful goddess. (Or a liar.) Emotional puppy crating isn't always feasible, and even when it is, it takes practice and concerted effort. Much like herding a twenty-pound package of muscle and saliva into a five-by-five cage, if you don't fasten the lock firmly enough, your emuppies could escape for a potentially destructive/exhausting scamper around your mental living room, scratching mental floors, chewing mental furniture, and further distracting you from calming the fuck down and dealing with your shit.

Who let the dogs out? You. You let them out.

That's okay. **You can always wrestle or gently lead or even trick them back in** — all tactics I'll explore and explain in part II. Like I said, *practice*. But it's worth it.

And don't forget: in the same way that you can lock those rascals up, you can also let them back out whenever you want.

Whenever you must.

Whenever their precious puppy faces will make you feel *better,* not worse.

It's not like you've sent your emotions to live with an elderly couple on a nice farm upstate. They're just chillin' in their crate until such time as they are once again invited to roam freely. When that time comes, go ahead, open the door. Let them romp around and entertain you for a spell, distract you from your woes, nuzzle your face, lick your toes. Whatever, I don't even have a dog, I'm just spitballing here.

But oh, hey! Once you've had your emotional puppy time, back in the crate they go.

Now be a good boy, and let's calm the fuck down.

CALM THE FUCK DOWN:
Identify what you can control,
accept what you can't,
and let that shit go

If part I was all about parameters, part II is all about practical application — the **how-tos for converting the what-ifs into the now-whats,** so to speak.

To ease you in, I'm going to focus mainly on **Shit That Hasn't Happened Yet** — the still-theoretical what-ifs, the kind of stuff that worries you whether or not it's even likely to occur. I'll help you determine if those worries are justified and if so, **how to prepare for and mitigate the damage** should the problems they stem from come to fruition.

And in some cases, **how to prevent those problems from happening at all.**

We'll start by **classifying your what-ifs by category,** much like the National Weather Service classifies hurricanes. Except in your case we're not dealing with hurricanes; we're dealing with…**shitstorms.**

Oh come on, you saw that pun coming a mile away.

Next, we'll assign a status — **prioritizing not only** *what* **needs dealing with, but** *how soon* — a calculation based on my very favorite factor: urgency.

At the end of part II, we'll use all of these tools to **mentally declutter your worryscape,** one hypothetical shitstorm at a time. And by practicing it on Shit That Hasn't Happened Yet, it'll be even easier to employ the NoWorries Method on Shit That Has Already Happened (coming right up in part III, natch).

Soon **you'll be turning what-ifs into now-whats like a pro.**

You won't even need me anymore. *Sniff.*

Pick a category, any category

As you probably know, hurricanes are categorized on a scale of 1 to 5. This is called the Saffir-Simpson Hurricane Wind Scale.

Those numbers are then used by meteorologists to forecast (and convey to you) the level of damage the storm is likely to inflict along its path, 1 being least severe, 5 being most. Of course, weatherpeople are not always correct — there are many unpredictable variables that determine the scope of the actual post-storm damage, such as the relative stability of the roofs, power lines, trees, awnings, boat docks, and lawn furniture in the affected area. (This is why weatherpeople have the best job security in all the land; it barely matters if they get it right all the time, because they *can't* get it right all the time and they seem totally okay with that. I would be a very bad weatherperson.)

But anyway, the 1–5 categories themselves are indisputable. They reflect the hurricane's strength in terms of its maximum sustained wind speed, which is a totally objective measurement. The anemometer don't lie.

Shitstorms are different in the sense that there is no "-ometer" that can measure the precise strength of any single event; **its strength, or what we'll term "severity," is informed solely by how the individual person affected *experiences it*.**

For example, say you've dreamt of playing Blanche Devereaux in *Thank You for Being a Friend: The Golden Girls Musical* for your entire life, but after a successful three-week run, you were unceremoniously kicked to the curb in favor of the director's new cougar girlfriend. You're devastated. On the other hand, your friend Guillermo is positively jubilant to have been let go from the funeral home where he was in charge of applying rouge and eye makeup to the clientele.

Same objective shitstorm, different subjective experience.

(Though maybe you could hook G up with the director's girlfriend? It would be a shame to let his talent for reanimating corpses go to waste.)

Further, you cannot compare your experience of any given shitstorm to anyone else's experience of a *different* shitstorm. Is your broken heart more or less "major" than my broken tooth? WHO CAN SAY.

Therefore, shitstorm categories are based not on *how severe* they might be — but simply *how likely* they are to actually hit you. One to five, on a scale of least to most probable. For example, if you're a popular person, then "What if nobody comes to my birthday party?" would be a **Category 1 Highly Unlikely**, whereas "What if two of my friends are having parties on the same weekend and I have to choose between them?" is a **Category 5 Inevitable.** Or vice versa, if you're a hermit.

From here on out, probability is your barometer. We'll call it, I don't know, your **probometer.**

And instead of having one weatherperson for the entire tri-state area charged with forecasting the accurate potential damage of a Category 3 storm passing over a thirteen-thousand-square-mile radius, who may or may not get it right when it comes to your house — we'll have one weatherperson focused *solely* on your house.

Oh, and your house is your life, and you are that weatherperson.

Actually, you're the "whetherperson," **because you and only you get to predict *whether* this shitstorm is likely to land on YOU.***

---

* These are the jokes, people.

The five categories on the Sarah Knight Shitstorm Scale are as follows:

Category 1: HIGHLY UNLIKELY

Category 2: POSSIBLE BUT NOT LIKELY

Category 3: LIKELY

Category 4: HIGHLY LIKELY

Category 5: INEVITABLE

Again, note that this scale indicates nothing of the "strength" or "severity" of the storm, merely the **probability of its occurrence**. When it comes to boarding up your metaphorical windows and battening down your metaphorical hatches, **your probometer rating will help you budget your freakout funds effectively.** Fewer FFs on less likely stuff, more on more likely stuff.

(And sometimes you won't need to spend any FFs at all on preparation; you can save them exclusively for cleanup. More on that later.)

To familiarize you with the category system, let's look at some potential shitstorms in action.

For example, do you ski? I don't, so it's HIGHLY UNLIKELY that I will break my leg skiing. Category 1, all the way. (Though if I *did* ski it would be Category 4 HIGHLY LIKELY that I would break my leg. I know my limits.)

Now consider Olympic gold medalist and nineties superhunk Alberto Tomba. Breaking his leg skiing might also be a HIGHLY UNLIKELY Category 1, because he's just that good. Or it might be a HIGHLY LIKELY Category 4 because he skis often, at high speeds, threading his obscenely muscled thighs between unforgiving metal structures. I leave it to Alberto in his capacity as his own personal whetherman to decide how likely *he* thinks it is that he'll break his leg skiing, and therefore how many (or few) freakout funds he needs to budget for that outcome on any given day.

Or, let's look at earthquakes. Those are fun.

People who live in Minnesota, which Wikipedia tells me is "not a very tectonically active state," are Category 1 HIGHLY UNLIKELY to experience a major earthquake; whereas homeowners along North America's Cascadia subduction zone are flirting with Category 5 every day. (Did you read that *New Yorker* article back in 2015, because I sure did. Sorry, Pacific Northwest, it was nice knowing you.) But that said, keep in mind that a Category 5 shitstorm doesn't have to be a catastrophic, earth-shaking event. **It is not necessarily all that *severe;* it is simply INEVITABLE.**

For example, if you're a parent, getting thrown up on is fully in the cards. If you're a female candidate for office, you'll be unfairly judged for your vocal timbre and wardrobe choices. And if you're a frequent flier, one of these days your connection will be delayed and leave you stranded in the Shannon, Ireland, airport for six hours with nothing but a complimentary ham sandwich and your laptop, on which you will watch *The Hateful Eight* and think, *Eh, it was just okay.*

Oh, and death is obviously a Category 5. It's gonna happen to all of us, our cats, dogs, hamsters, and annual plants.

Can I get a downgrade?

Each what-if is like a tropical cyclone brewing on the radar screen of your mind. A shitclone, as it were. Some will turn into full-fledged shitstorms and some won't — but unlike tropical cyclones, you may have control over the direction your shitclones take. Especially the Category 1s, since they're highly unlikely as it is. For example, if I continue to never go skiing, I will NEVER break my leg skiing. Crisis completely and totally averted! Yeah, yeah, I heard you groan, but that was a freebie. I can't give away my best stuff this early. Later in part II, we'll discuss less ridiculously restrictive but equally effective ways to send a shitstorm out to sea. Promise.

Mulling the likelihood of a potential shitstorm actually coming to pass is a useful exercise. Consulting your probometer helps you focus on the reality of your situation instead of obsessing over what-ifs that are often as unrealistic as the "after" photos in an ad for cut-rate diet pills. You know she just went for a spray tan, sucked in her stomach, and tricked out the tatas in a more flattering bra. Stop falling for that shit, will ya?

And by the way, I apologize if all this talk of impending doom is triggering a freakout, but it's for the best. **Because when you start thinking about shitstorms based on probability, you'll begin to realize you don't have nearly as much to worry about as you thought you did.**

Soon, when a what-if pops up on your radar screen you'll be able to say, "Total Cat. One. Not worth worrying about." Or "Category Two, no need to spend those freakout funds quite yet."

LOGIC CAN BE VERY SOOTHING.

Logicats, ho!

Speaking of logic, from here on out, I'm going to see your emotional puppies and raise you some cold, hard logical cats. Think about it: a puppy will flail around in the yard trying to scratch his back on a busted Frisbee, whereas cats can reach their own backs and, generally speaking, they're not much for flailing. Dogs are players — giddily chasing a ball one minute, then getting distracted by a body of water that needs splashing in. Cats are hunters — approaching their target with laser focus and pouncing (it must be said) with catlike reflexes. They are the official spirit animal of *Calm the Fuck Down*.

The gathering shitstorms: a list

You may already know this about me, but I fucking love a list.

In this section, and in keeping with what I asked you to do back in part I, I'm going to **name some of my what-ifs — the** things that wake me up in a panic or keep me from fully enjoying my afternoon spritz — so I can figure out which resultant worries deserve my attention and which ones I can discard, then start organizing my response to the rest.

Lists, man. Lists give me life!

For now, I'll stick with **Shit That Hasn't Happened Yet** because it's easier to practice on a theoretical. Fear not, though — we'll deal with **Shit That Has Already Happened** a bit later in the book.

10 WHAT-IFS I MAY OR MAY NOT NEED TO WORRY ABOUT

- My house key gets stuck in the door
- A palm tree falls on my roof
- More tarantulas appear in my house
- I get into a car accident on the winding mountain road to the airport
- It rains on my day off that I wanted to spend at the beach
- My cats die
- I order a different pizza than usual and it isn't very good
- My editor hates this chapter
- I show up for a speaking gig and totally bomb

- I ruin my favorite pineapple-print shorts by sitting in something nasty

Now I'm going to ask you to make your own list of what-ifs. Like mine, they should be drawn from **Shit That Hasn't Happened Yet.**

If you are a generally anxious person who has also been known to gaze into a clear blue sky and imagine a plane falling out of it and onto your hammock, this should be an easy exercise.

If you consider yourself merely **situationally anxious — worrying about shit only if and when it happens** — I envy you, buddy. But I still want you to make a list, because it doesn't really matter whether every time you sit in the chair you're worried the barber is going to cut it too short. One of these days, he may slip up and give you an unintentional asymmetrical fade, and you'll have to calm the fuck down and deal with it — the strategy for which is the same for all of us. Use your imagination.

10 WHAT-IFS I MAY OR MAY NOT NEED TO WORRY ABOUT

_____	_____
_____	_____
_____	_____

_____   _____

_____   _____

Next, we're going to bust out our probometers and **categorize each of these potential shitstorms by probability.** Looking at problems rationally and based on all available data — like your friendly neighborhood weatherperson would look at them — helps you budget your freakout funds effectively.

I'll annotate my list/categorizations so you can follow my train of thought.

10 WHAT-IFS I MAY OR MAY NOT NEED TO WORRY ABOUT: RANKED BY PROBABILITY

- **My house key gets stuck in the door**
  Cat. 2 — POSSIBLE BUT NOT LIKELY

It may seem trivial, but I worry about this because it happened once before and my husband had to climb a ladder and go in through a window, which made us realize how unsecured our windows were, so now we've installed locks on those. Therefore, if my key gets stuck in the door again, *I'll* be stuck outside with the mosquitos waiting for a locksmith, which, per earlier, is a dangerous game in this town. Since we never figured out why it got stuck that one time, I have to assume it could happen again. However, the ratio is like, one thousand door unlockings to one stuck key, so probability remains low.*

- **A palm tree falls on my roof**
  Cat. 2 — POSSIBLE BUT NOT LIKELY

There are only two palm trees within striking distance of our house, and we had two *actual* Category 5 hurricanes pass over our town in two weeks last summer. So far, so good. Then again, climate change. I'll give it a 2.

- **More tarantulas appear in my house**
  Cat. 1 — HIGHLY UNLIKELY

I've been here several years and seen exactly one tarantula. On a day-to-day basis, this is a technical 1, even if it's an emotional 5. Emuppies, in the crate you go. Logicats, be on the lookout, 'kay?

- **I get into a car accident on the winding mountain road to the airport**
  Cat. 2 — POSSIBLE BUT NOT LIKELY

I had to think a little harder about this one — you often do, when the worries are about really bad potential shit. My first instinct was to call it a Cat. 4 Highly Likely simply because every single time I get in that taxi I fear for my life. But I'm a nervous passenger,

---

* I guess I technically broke my own rule about Shit That Hasn't Happened Yet. Whatever, it's my book.

equally terrified on third world dirt roads and well-maintained five-lane highways in developed countries. And if we've all been paying attention, we know that our level of anxiety *about* the problem doesn't predict the *probability of the problem occurring.* I can't bring myself to call it "highly unlikely" (I've seen, um, a few accidents on the way to the airport); however, "possible but not likely" feels both accurate and manageably stressful.

- **It rains on my day off that I wanted to spend at the beach**
  Cat. 4 — HIGHLY LIKELY

I'm not making this up for effect — it is currently raining (and has been all morning) *while* the sun is shining brightly. I will never understand this form of tropical shower. WHERE IS THE RAIN COMING FROM?

- **My cats die**
  Cat. 5 — INEVITABLE

Cats are fascinating, crafty beasts, but they are not immortal. (I suppose there's a small chance that Gladys and/or Mister Stussy will outlive *me,* but that's a Category 1.)

- **I order a different pizza than usual and it isn't very good**
  Cat. 1 — HIGHLY UNLIKELY

I'm a creature of habit *and* I'm very good at predicting what toppings will work in harmony on a pizza. Get to know me.

- **My editor hates this chapter**
  Cat. 1 — HIGHLY UNLIKELY

Like driving the winding mountain road, this is a situation where my innate anxiety initially compels me to forecast a more severe shitstorm than is on the radar. When in truth, it is neither inevitable nor even highly likely that my editor will hate this chapter. We must use all available data to make our predictions. And Mike? He's a lover, not a hater.

- **I show up for a speaking gig and totally bomb**
  Cat. 2 — POSSIBLE BUT NOT LIKELY

Again, setting aside the anxious emotions and focusing on the raw data, I have done a fair amount of public speaking and I have never once bombed. But there's no point in jinxing it, so we'll call this a 2.

- **I ruin my favorite pineapple-print shorts by sitting in something nasty**
  Cat. 3 — LIKELY

In my new hometown, it's nearly impossible not to sit in something nasty at one point or another — be it dirt, sand, a squashed bug, animal poop, motor oil, or an old wet cigar. With indoor/outdoor living comes schmutz. With tourists comes litter. With drunk people and children come spills. Ah, island life. I used to think I could keep this brand of shitstorm to a Category 1 if I just didn't wear my favorite shorts whenever I went to…oh, right. Everywhere I go is schmutz waiting to happen. Sigh. On the bright side, I have a washing machine and I know how to use it! Category 3 it is.

<table>
<tr><td>

Category key

1. HIGHLY
   UNLIKELY
2. POSSIBLE BUT
   NOT LIKELY
3. LIKELY
4. HIGHLY LIKELY
5. INEVITABLE

</td></tr>
</table>

Looking over my annotated list, you'll see that out of ten random things I have been known to worry about— **and that haven't even happened yet**— three of them are Category 1 Highly Unlikely. That's 33.3 percent of my shit off the screens, right there.

Another four of them are Category 2 Possible But Not Likely. We are now more than halfway through my what-ifs and they're dropping like flies in the champagne room.

I don't know about you, but I'm feeling calmer already.

So, are you hip to categorizing your own list? I'll give you extra space to jot down your thought process like I did—because sometimes you have to explain yourself *to* yourself before either of you can understand where you're coming from.

10 WHAT-IFS I MAY OR MAY NOT
NEED TO WORRY ABOUT:
RANKED BY PROBABILITY

Category: _____   Category: _____

Category: _____   Category: _____

Category: _____   Category: _____

Category: _____   Category: _____

Category: _____   Category: _____

Without being there to look over your shoulder or knowing you personally (Well, most of you. Hi, Dave!), I'm guessing that a solid chunk of your what-if list is populated by Category 1s and 2s like mine was, which you can and should stop worrying about posthaste. Later in part II, I'll show you how to do just that. (Hint: it involves the One Question to Rule Them All.)

And even if you're a little heavier on the 3s, 4s, and 5s, you're about to pick up a whole lotta new strategies for weathering shitstorms by **discarding** **unproductive worries and** **organizing** **a productive response.**

Mental decluttering. I'm telling you, it's the tits.

What's your status?

Once you have logically, rationally determined that a what-if is a probable shitstorm, a useful follow-up question is **"How *soon* is it going to land?"**

There are three levels of urgency:

OUTLYING

An outlying shitstorm not only hasn't happened, you can't even be sure if it will. Theoretically, these should be the easiest to stop worrying about because they are both unlikely *and* distant — low pressure and low priority. Ironic, since low-pressure situations are what create legit rainstorms, but once again, metaphors and the anti-gurus who employ them are imperfect.

IMMINENT

Imminent shitstorms also haven't happened yet, but they're more solidly formed and you're likely to know if and when they'll hit. You still might be

---

Examples of outlying shitstorms

You might lose the election next year.

You might not get promoted as fast as you wanted to.

You might hurt yourself training for a marathon.

You might never hear back from that girl you met at the bar.

You might not lose the weight in time for the class reunion.

You might follow in your parents' footsteps and need cataract surgery someday.

You might get beaten to that patent by a fellow inventor.

---

able to prevent an imminent shitstorm, but if not, at least you can prep for impact and mitigate the fallout.

TOTAL

A total shitstorm is one that is already upon you. You might've seen it coming when it was still imminent, or it may have appeared out of nowhere like some twelve-year-old YouTuber who has more followers than Islam and Christianity combined. It matters not whether the effects of the storm would be considered mild or severe (by you or anyone else) — it's here, and you have to deal with it.

Whether the shitstorm is a Highly Unlikely Category 1 or an Inevitable 5 — **if it hasn't happened yet, you can worry about it less urgently than if it's just about to or if it just did.**

Got it?

Examples of imminent shitstorms

You might lose the election *tomorrow*.

You might not hit your 5:00 p.m. deadline.

You might fail your history exam on Monday.

You might get in trouble for that inappropriate joke you made in the meeting.

You might not qualify for the mortgage.

You might miss your tight connection in Philly.

If she sees you leaving the building on her way in, your sister might find out you slept with her boyfriend.

The more the hairier

Okay, but what happens if you have *multiple* storms on the radar and you're reasonably confident you're going to need to spend time, energy, and/or money worrying about/dealing with all of them?

There's a reason the phrase is "mo' money, mo' problems," not "mo' problems, mo' money." You don't get a magical influx of freakout funds just because you've had a magical influx of shit land in your lap. **Keep using urgency as a tool for determining the prioritization of withdrawals.**

Here's a little quiz:

1. **You fucked up at work, but your boss doesn't know it yet because she's on vacation for two weeks.**

   Category: _____
   Status: _____

2. **Your wife is 9.2 months pregnant.**

   Category: _____
   Status: _____

3. **This is a two-parter:**

a. **Your car is a relatively new make and reliable model. What if it breaks down?**

   Category: _____
   Status: _____

b. **Surprise! It just broke down.**

   Category: _____
   Status: _____

ANSWERS:

1. **Category 4 Highly Likely / Outlying Shitstorm**
   (Also acceptable: Category 3 Likely / Outlying)

You're pretty sure your boss is going to tear you a new one when she gets back. However, it's going to be at least two weeks, which is in no way "imminent." So much other shit could happen in two weeks — including your boss acquiring more urgent fires to put out than yelling at or firing *you*. (I'm not saying go full ostrich — just pointing out that the time to deal with your boss being mad at you is if/when you know your boss is actually mad at you. Maybe she'll be too blissed out from her Peruvian ayahuasca retreat to even notice what you did.)

Save your freakout funds for now. Especially since (a) you can't do anything about the fact that you already fucked up and (b) you might need that time and energy later to beg for-giveness or update your résumé.

2.   Category 5 Inevitable / Imminent Shitstorm

That baby is coming soon and you know it. You have no con-trol over when or how, but you can do a little prep to make life easier in the eventual moment.

A prudent withdrawal of FFs is in order. Prepare for landfall by spending some time, energy, and money putting together a go bag, stocking the freezer with ready-made meals, and sleeping — because once that kid arrives it's all over between you and Mr. Sandman.

3a.   Category 1 Highly Unlikely / Outlying Shitstorm

3b.   Category 1 Highly Unlikely / Total Shitstorm

Based on the information contained in the first part of the question, this should have been an easy Category 1. But as we know, SHIT HAPPENS — even, sometimes, the highly unlikely shit — and when its status leaps from outlying to total, you have to deal with it in a *higher-priority* fashion than either of the other two storms on the radar.

Prioritizing based on urgency. BOOM.

You're going to need a car to drive yourself to work for the last two weeks that you definitely still have a job, and to drive Margaret to the hospital sometime, well, imminently.

Withdraw FFs immediately. Call a mechanic and see about getting your Volvo towed over to the garage, then call Hertz to see about a rental to tide you over.

Oh, wait, what was that? Margaret's water just broke? Fuck. Another total shitstorm! In this particular case it doesn't take a genius to determine that the one raining down amniotic fluid upon you and your sofa is the one you need to worry about first. Margaret's comfort takes priority, and you can deal with your car sitch whenever there's a break in the action.*

Time to reprioritize. Instead of a mechanic, you're calling an Uber. And a cleaning service.

Choose it or lose it

When more than one shitstorm is vying for top priority, pick one to focus on *for now*. You can always switch back and forth, but if you try to do simultaneous double duty, you'll blow through your freakout funds faster than Johnny Depp through a pile of Colombian marching powder, and lose your goddamn mind while you're at it. I can see it now — you'll be trying to change Margaret's fan belt and begging the mechanic for an epidural in an absurd Cockney pirate accent. If you want to stay sane, pick a lane.

---

* Hahaha you're about to have a baby. There won't be a break in the action for eighteen years.

EXTRA CREDIT QUIZ QUESTION: You get lost while hiking in the Sierra Madres (total shitstorm) and then you break your toe on a big stupid rock (total shitstorm *numero dos*) just as a rescue helicopter is circling overhead. Do you spend your time and energy wrapping your broken toe, or jumping up and down on it waving your only survival flare in hopes of flagging down your ride to the nearest ER?

Answer: P-R-I-O-R-I-T-I-Z-E. Jump for your life! Signal the chopper! (And carry more than one survival flare, kids. Safety first.)

To recap: When it comes to outlying, imminent, or total shitstorms, how do you prepare?

- Make like a weatherperson and forecast outcomes based on all available data.

- Ask yourself not only *How likely is this to happen to me?* but also *How soon?*

- And before you spend your freakout funds, ask yourself the One Question to Rule Them All: *Can I control it?*

Get ur control freak on

In this section I'll take you through a practice round of "Can I control it?" But first, I want to examine **the different *kinds* of control you may or may not be able to exert on any given situation.** It's a sliding scale, and you'd be well served to understand the nuances.

> **Out of your hands:** These are the things you can't control at all — such as the weather, other people's actions, the number of hours in a day, and the number of chances your boyfriend is going to give you before he gets sick of your *What if he's cheating on me* bullshit and dumps you anyway because you're needy and untrusting.*
>
> **Make a contribution:** You can't control the larger underlying problem, but you can do your part to minimize its effects. For example, in terms of the weather, you can't control the rain, but you can control *whether* or not you suffer its effects to the fullest if you bring an umbrella. You can't control the number of hours in a day, but you can control *whether* you spend too many of them watching online contouring tutorials instead of hand-washing your delicates like you should be. And you

---

* This Category 4 goes out to a Twitter follower who seems both admirably self-aware and destined to remain single forever.

can't control Randy's ultimate level of tolerance for your "WHO IS SHE???" comments on his Facebook page, but you can control *whether* you keep using your fingers to tap out those three little words. (Or you could just break up with Randy because, let's face it, where there's smoke there's fire.)

Under your influence: This stuff, you can *heavily influence* if not completely control — such as "not oversleeping," by way of setting an alarm. Is it possible that something will prevent your alarm from going off (like a power outage or a mouse gnawing through the wire), or you from heeding its siren song (like accidentally pressing OFF instead of SNOOZE)? Sure, but that's a Category 1 Highly Unlikely Shitstorm and you know it. Or…am I to infer from this line of questioning that you don't really *want* to calm the fuck down?

Uh-huh. Carry on.

Complete control: This is shit you are always 100 percent in control of, such as "the words that come out of your mouth" and "whether or not you are wearing pants."

As I have stated and will continue to drill into your skull like an old-timey lobotomist, **worrying is a waste of your precious time, energy, and money. And worrying about things you CAN'T CONTROL is the biggest waste of all.** This is true of low-level anxieties and high-probability shitstorms, from existential angst to all-out catastrophes. Whether they be problems with your friends, family, boss, coworkers, car, bank account, boyfriend, girlfriend, or tarantulas — the ones you have the power to solve, the worries YOU can discard and the responses YOU can organize are the ones to focus on.

The One Question to Rule Them All, in action

- **What if I tell my bestie Rachel what I really think of her new bangs and she never forgives me?**

Can I control it? Completely. Keep your trap shut and your friendship intact.

Or:

- **What if I accidentally shout another woman's name in bed with my new girlfriend?**

Can I control it? Yes. For God's sake, Randy, get ahold of yourself. No wonder your new girlfriend doesn't trust you.

How about:

- **What if rumors of a union dispute come to pass and force the cancellation of that monster truck rally next Wednesday that I was all excited about?**

Can I control it? Unless you also happen to be the Monster Truckers Union president, unequivocally no. Which means that this is a worry you should ideally DISCARD. (I'll move on to "Okay, but *how* do I discard it?" in a few. Be patient — it's not like you have a monster truck rally to attend.)

Or:

- **What if something bad happens to people I give incorrect directions to?**

Can I control it? Yes, by telling the next nice young couple from Bismarck that you have a terrible sense of geography and they'd be better off querying a fire hydrant. This what-if is supremely easy to snuff out in its inception — take it from someone who thinks turning right automatically means going "east."

And sometimes, you might have to **break a big worry down into smaller components** — some of which you can control and some of which you can't.

- **What if I laugh so hard I pee my pants during my friend's stand-up gig?**

Can I control it? First of all, lucky you if your stand-up comedian friend is actually that funny. If you're prone to laugh-leaks, you may not be able to control the bladder, but you can make a contribution to your overall preparedness. There are many options in the personal hygiene aisle that were invented expressly to assist you in dealing with this issue.

This is so much fun, I think we should try a few more — this time, on what-ifs pulled directly from the pulsating brains of my Twitter followers.

Shit people in my Twitter feed are worried about. Can they control it?

- **I'm happy and in a good relationship, but what if we wait too long to get married and never have kids?**

Can I control it? This is one you can heavily influence. You don't necessarily have full control over whether you get pregnant, but in terms of this specific what-if, you *can* control "not waiting too long" to start trying. You know how this whole aging eggs thing works, and if you have to, you can explain it to Dan. However, if you have to explain it to Dan...maybe Dan should have paid more attention in tenth-grade bio.

- **What if I never find the escape hatch from my soul-sucking day job?**

Can I control it? Yes. You can only never find what you stop looking for. I think it was Yoda who said that. Bit of an anti-guru himself, that guy.

- **What if I'm failing as an adult?**

Can I control it? Yes. Adults do things like pay taxes, take responsibility for their actions, make their own dinner, and show up on time for prostate exams. Do these things and you will be succeeding as an adult. If your what-if is more existential in nature, perhaps you should get a hobby. Adults have those, too.

- **What if I choose not to go home and visit my family this weekend and something bad happens to them and then I regret it forever?**

Can I control it? Yes. If your goal is not to have to worry about this, go visit them. If what you're really asking for is permission to not drive six hours to DC in holiday-weekend traffic and you *also* don't want to worry about the consequences of that decision, bust out your trusty probometer. How likely is it that something bad is going to happen to your family, this weekend of all weekends? It's a Category 1, isn't it? You know what to do.

- **What if my son doesn't have the developmental problems his doctors think he has and he's just a budding sociopath?**

Can I control it? Yikes. I'm sorry to say, you can't control *whether* the kid's a sociopath. You can't even heavily influence it, if we're talking a DNA-level shitstorm. But you can contribute to the overall cause by continuing to seek help for him.

(And maybe a second opinion while you're at it. Seems prudent in this case.)

- **What if all my friends secretly hate me and I don't know it?**

Can I control it? I refer you to your internal whetherperson to determine the probability of this scenario. Assemble all the available data. If your friends are nice to you on a regular basis and don't avoid your calls or talk shit about you in group chats that they think you're not going to see except they don't know that Sondra is always leaving her phone unlocked and sitting on the table when she goes to pee, then they probably don't hate you. If they *do* do these things, I don't think they're keeping it much of a secret? I'm not sure I understand the question.

- **What if I have an ugly baby?**

Can I control it? No. And besides, all babies are ugly. You're not going to get a real sense of how that thing turned out until much later in life, and even then, puberty does terrible things to a human.

- **What if democracy is failing and my kids are in mortal danger because of that?**

Can I control it? Not really. But please vote. Or run for office. We all need you.

- **What if I get laid off without warning?**

Can I control it? Being laid off? As in not fired, but rather let go without cause, and as you said, "without warning"? No. (Come on, the answer was right there in the question!) On the other hand, if you're asking what if you get *fired* without warning, well, I bet that if your boss plans on firing you, he or she has actually given you plenty of warning—you just weren't listening.

- **What if my aging parents start to fall apart?**

Can I control it? Ultimately, no. You can encourage them to get checkups and fill prescriptions and maybe sign up for a light water aerobics class to stay limber, but you're not in control of anyone else's health or related decision-making. If they do go ahead and fall apart, you can worry about it then.

- **What if I get bitten by a raccoon?**

Can I control it? Yes. By not hanging out with raccoons. Who are you, Davy Crockett?

Last but not least, a query that stood out to me for an oddly personal reason:

- **What if my teeth fall out?**

Can I control it? You can heavily influence your teeth staying put by brushing regularly, swigging mouthwash, flossing (eh), going to the dentist, wearing a night guard, and steering clear of ice hockey and guys named Wonka. However, this particular tweet gave me pause not because I'm consciously worried about the fate of my bicuspids, but because I happen to have a teeth-falling-out dream every few months. And when I looked it up in one of those dream interpretation books I learned that lost or crumbling teeth in your dream indicates a feeling of powerlessness in real life. In other words, a loss of control. Apparently my anxiety runs so deep, I'm what-iffing in my sleep. So meta!

If the answer is no, this is how you let it go

What may come as a surprise to you after reading the previous section is that NONE OF THIS SHOULD COME AS A SURPRISE TO YOU.

Can you control it (or aspects of it) — yes or no? You already have the answers, friend.

We've established that you cannot, for example, *control* being suddenly laid off. But if you're worried about this, I understand where you're coming from. Throughout my twenties, my ability to perform my job well was not in question. I was not in danger of getting fired for cause. Still, I worried passionately about losing my job due to cutbacks or other factors at the corporate level that I definitely could not control.

I remember having these worries. I remember people telling me that everything would be fine and that I couldn't control it anyway, so I should let it go and stop freaking out about it.

And I remember thinking EASY FOR YOU TO SAY, JERK-FACE McGEE.

Or, as one of my Twitter followers more politely articulated, **"How do I get from understanding that worry is pointless to** *actually not worrying?*"

Excellent question. Once you've ACKNOWLEDGED the problem, you begin to let go of your worries about said problem by ACCEPTING the things you can't control—a skill that over 60 percent of my anonymous survey takers have yet to master, by the by.

I hope that the same 60 percent are reading, because it's actually easier to do than they—or you—might think.

Reality check, please!

Please note: I am not using the word "acceptance" in the sense that you're supposed to suddenly become *happy* about whatever shit has happened that you can't control. It's totally understandable—especially in the short term—to be very fucking upset by shit we can't control, as Ross was when Rachel broke up with him on *Friends* using the very words "Accept that."*

But if you've been dumped, duped, or dicked over, facts are facts. Continuing to spend time, energy, and/or money — in the long term — being anxious, sad, or angry about it (or avoiding it) is a waste of freakout funds.

Girl, don't act like you don't know this. We've been over it multiple times.

For the purposes of this book and execution of the NoWorries Method, **I'm using the word "accept" to mean "understand the reality of the situation."**

That's not so hard, is it? If you can accept that the sky is blue and water is wet and macarons are disappointing and borderline fraudulent as a dessert, you can accept the things you can't control.

And when you answer the One Question to Rule Them All with a *No*, you have *already* accepted reality. You have admitted that you can't control something — it's that simple. HUZZAH! Sarah Knight, dropping commonsense knowledge bombs since 2015.

---

* From "The One the Morning After."

Let's be real

A frequent precursor to the Freakout Faces is an inability to accept reality. In one sense, you may be worrying about something that hasn't even happened yet, which means it is literally not yet "real." A what-if exists in your imagination; only when it becomes real is it a problem you can acknowledge, accept, and address. Or you may be freaking out because you can't force the outcome you want, e.g., one that is not "realistic." I'll go over that more in part III, in the section aptly titled "Identify your realistic ideal outcome." Meanwhile, chew on this:

The path from what-ifs and worrying to calming the fuck down is a straight line from "things that exist in your imagination" to "things that exist in reality" and then "accepting those things as reality."

Maybe reread that a few times just to be sure you're smelling what I'm cooking. In fact, see the next page for a graphic you can photocopy and keep in your wallet or bring down to Spike at the Sweet Needle so he can tattoo it across your chest for daily reaffirmation.

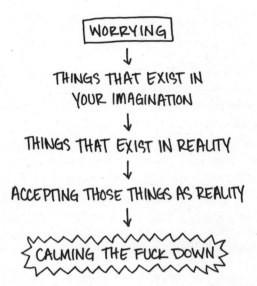

And just like that, you've nearly calmed the fuck down — all that remains to complete Step 1 of the NoWorries Method is to DISCARD that unrealistic, unproductive worry like the good little mental declutterer I know you can be.

To do that, you have a couple of options.

Option 1: Just fucking let it go

You still think it's easier said than done? Fine. But I encourage you to consider everything we've talked about so far and apply your new tools and perspective on a case-by-case basis.

For example, if you're working those shitstorm categories like I taught you, you should be able to reduce your worry load immediately, and significantly.

If something is highly unlikely to happen, why are you worrying about it?

And if it's far off in the distance, why are you worrying about it NOW?

Oh, and is this something you can control? No? Hm. Then there's no reason you should be spending your precious time, energy, and money on it at all.

Seems pretty straightforward, doesn't it? Like...maybe the kind of stuff you should already know?

Well, I think you DO know it, somewhere in your palpitating heart of hearts—I'm just helping you access that knowledge. No shame in a little teamwork. I've found that in times of stress, people can't always make the commonsense connections that others can make *for* them, if others are granted a reasonable deadline and unlimited Doritos to sit down at their laptop and spell it all out.

It's a symbiotic relationship, yours and mine.

Which is to say, I'm not at all surprised that you couldn't just fucking let go of any of your worries before you picked up this book—but I'd be really surprised if by now, you can't just fucking let go of, like, a bunch of them.

Option 2: Houdini that shit

Unlike Bryan Cranston, whose character starts out enraged by but eventually comes to like the guy who's trying to marry his onscreen daughter in the criminally underrated movie *Why Him?*, you cannot count on becoming happy about the thing that, right now, has you very fucking upset.

But you CAN become happy (or calm or proactive, etc.), right now, about *something else* entirely — which in turn causes you to stop worrying about the original thing.

Ta-daaa! I call this technique **"sleight of mind."**

It's like when I'm freaking out about a deadline, so I go for a bracing dip in the pool to clear my head. That doesn't change the fact of five thousand words being due in someone's inbox tomorrow, but it does temporarily change my focus from *I'm a fraud and will never write another syllable* to *Ooh, that feels nice.*

Just like sleight of hand enables a magician to perform his thrilling act, sleight of mind is how we'll make your worries disappear — at least temporarily, and maybe even for good. (And don't come at me with "That's cheating!" I promised you tricks all the way back on page one. You should really start taking me at my word.)

Now, recall, if you would, the Flipsides of the Four Faces of Freaking Out:

ANXIOUS?	→	FOCUS
SAD?	→	REPAIR WITH SELF-CARE
ANGRY?	→	PEACE OUT WITH PERSPECTIVE
AVOIDING?	→	ACT UP

This is where the magic happens, people. I now present you with a collection of simple, elegant tricks you can tuck up your voluminous sleeve for when the worrying gets tough and the tough need to STOP WORRYING.*

How to stop being anxious about something

The what-ifs are multiplying on the radar screen. Your nerves are frayed, your teeth are ground to nubs, and you can't stop over-thinking whatever shit is about to go or has gone down.

You need to FOCUS, Jim! (On something else.)

GIVE ANXIETY THE FINGER(S)

When I'm anxious, I walk around the house wiggling my digits like I'm playing air piano or doing low-key jazz hands. My hus-

---

* For linguistic continuity with the NoWorries Method, I use "worrying" here to mean "any way in which you are exhibiting the signs of a freakout."

band calls them my "decluttering fingers" since they always signal a prelude to some semimanic tidying. But in addition to clearing out the kitchen cabinets or denuding the coffee table of old magazines, what I'm doing is temporarily channeling my anxiety into something productive and, to me, comforting.

You may not be as into tidying-as-therapy, but surely there's another hands-on task you enjoy that you could turn to when you feel your Anxious face settling in around the temples. Perhaps industriously restringing your guitar, mending a pair of pants, or repairing the teeny-tiny trundle bed in your kid's dollhouse. (It's probably time to admit it's *your* dollhouse, Greg.)*

GET DOWN WITH O.P.P.

Other people's problems, that is. Maybe you don't have an on-call therapist — but you've got friends, family, neighbors, and the guy down at the post office with the beard that looks like it rehomes geese who got lost on their way south for the winter. Chat 'em up. Ask your sister how she's doing and listen to *her* shit. Release some of your anxiety by giving her advice that you should probably be taking your own damn self.

It's harder to stay anxious about any particular thing when you don't allow yourself the mental space to dwell on it — and a darn good

---

* Someone who was anxious about finishing her book on time may also have pruned a gigantic papyrus bush with a pair of kitchen scissors today.

way to accomplish that is by filling said space with conversation, human interaction, and *other people's* problems. How do you think I stay so calm these days? I spend all year giving you advice.

Tonight You, meet Tomorrow You

This seems like a good place to address the tarantula in the room, which is that when anxiety is keeping you up at night, you may be able to name your problem (Good job!), but you can't necessarily solve it in the moment.

I get that, which is why I want to take a moment to introduce you to one of my favorite mental magician-and-assistant duos: **Tonight You and Tomorrow You.**

Let's say it is currently 3:00 a.m. on Friday, and you can't sleep because on Tuesday you made an offhand comment to your coworker Ruth that you're worried she may have interpreted as an insult even though she didn't give any indication of such at the time and even though not one single word that came out of your mouth could possibly, by any sentient being, be thought of as a criticism.

Still. *What if?!?*

Well, if it's 3:00 a.m., then Tonight You CAN'T call Ruth and CAN'T tell her you hope she wasn't offended by that thing you said and CAN'T feel better about it when she replies, "What? I don't even remember you saying that, so obviously I was not offended, you silly goose."

But **Tonight You CAN set Tomorrow You up for success —** by getting some goddamn sleep, Chief.

You may think it's impossible to fall asleep when you're anxious about making things right with Ruth or when your to-do list is scrolling through your mind on endless loop like the NASDAQ on Times Square, **but hear me out — this might be the single most useful nugget in this entire compendium of calm.**

First, think of the problem in terms of what we've discussed thus far:

Falling asleep is the more urgent issue, so it should be your priority, right? *Check.*

Furthermore, it's the only part of this equation you have some control over now, *and* it's one you can actually solve, correct? *Check plus.*

This is reality. Can you accept it? *Checkmate.*

Ah, but not so fast, eh? I can smell your annoyance from here — a heady musk of *Fuck you* with a hint of *Don't patronize me, lady.* Do you feel like you're being bullied into doing something you simply cannot do, even though you know it's good for you? I get that, too. For whatever reason, sometimes taking good, solid advice from other people is impossible. Definitely an occupational hazard for *moi.*

So let's look at your problem another way. Say, through the lens of my early twenties — a time when my then-boyfriend, now-husband's entreaties for me to hydrate after every third cocktail felt more like a scolding than a suggestion, and when *even though I knew he was right,* I didn't like feeling pressured, condescended to, or preshamed for tomorrow's hangover. Nope, there was no better way to activate the You-Can't-Make-Me Face than to tell Sarah Knight a few V&Ts in that she "should drink some water."

Did I regret it in the morning? Yes. Did I take his advice next time? No. 'Twas a vicious cycle, with extra lime.

Then one blessed day, a friend introduced me to the concept of a "spacer," and everything changed. This was not a stupid glass of stupid water that somebody else *told* me to drink. No, it's a spacer! It has a fun name! And I get to control my own narrative by sidling up to the bar and ordering one. My spacer, my choice.

Where the fuck, you may by now be thinking, *is she going with this?*

Well, besides having just introduced you to the second-most-useful nugget in this entire book, I would argue that deciding to have oneself a spacer is similar to deciding to go to sleep. In terms of being in a state where you know what you should be doing but don't appreciate being told to do it, "intoxicated" is quite similar to "whipped into an anxious, insomniac frenzy," is it not?

I take your point. But what if I just can't fall asleep, even though I agree that it's best for me?

Good, I'm glad we're getting somewhere. Because I think—based on extensive personal experience—that you CAN drift off to dreamland if you approach the task differently than you have been thus far. If you take control of the narrative. If you treat "going to sleep" like ordering a spacer or checking off an item on that scrolling to-do list. Set your mind to accomplishing it and therefore to *feeling accomplished* instead of feeling like a very tired failure.

But you're not going to be there to remind me of this helpful nugget every night when my brain goes into overdrive—and even if you were, you still sound kind of smugly self-satisfied about the whole thing, tbh.

Noted. But remember Tonight You and Tomorrow You? They've been waiting in the wings for the grand finale...

One night as I was tossing and turning like one of those Chinese fortune-telling fish, my husband looked at me and said, **"Tonight Sarah's job is to go to sleep. Tomorrow Sarah can deal with this shit tomorrow."**

So I thought about it that way, and I gave Tonight Me her marching orders.

And it worked!

Maybe he adapted it from the spacer trick when he saw how well that penetrated my defenses, or maybe I married a goddamn wizard, but I don't care either way because ever since, I've been able to reframe the I-can't-fall-asleep conversation—with MYSELF—and **shift my focus from not being able to do the only thing I so badly *want* to do, to doing the only thing I *can* do.**

> **Other ways to reduce anxiety that I didn't invent but that have been known to work**
>
> Deep breaths. In through the nose, out through the mouth.
> Yoga
> Sex
> Bubble baths
> Counting slowly to one hundred
> Magnesium supplements
> Adult coloring books

And you know, I've always trusted Tomorrow Me to handle tomorrow's tasks, assuming she gets enough shut-eye. Now I recognize that it's Tonight Me's job to get her to the starting line in fine fettle.

Talk about sleight of mind. Yep. Definitely married a wizard.

But hey, you don't have to take it from us. Take it from Tonight You — Tomorrow You will thank you tomorrow.

How to stop being sad about something

What's another word for grieving, blue, mopey, forlorn, despondent, and depressed? HURTING. You're hurting. So you need to heal. Grant yourself a reasonable amount of time and energy to be sad about whatever shit has you worried and weepy.

Then, crate your emotional puppies and stave off the prolonged wallowing with a shot of SELF-CARE.

LAUGHTER IS THE BEST MEDICINE

Much like "Calm the fuck down," the phrase "Turn that frown upside down" is advice not often well received by a person who is midfreakout. I know that, but I'll say it anyway, because that shit *works*. For example, when I'm feeling utterly dejected, a certain someone's patented C + C Music Factory tribute dance/lip sync always brings me back from the brink. If something has you down, seek help from things that reliably cheer you up. Cat pics. Videos of people coming out of anesthesia. Perhaps an aptly termed "feel-good movie"? Anything in the *Pitch Perfect* oeuvre applies.

Even if this trick stops you worrying for only the length of one song (in my case, "Things That Make You Go Hmmm…")—you've stopped, haven't you? Progress!

YOU'RE IN FOR A TREAT

When someone else is sad, be they grieving or recuperating, you might stop by with some prepared food to get them over the hump—casserole, cookies, a fruit basket. Why not show yourself the same kindness? Your treat doesn't have to be food-based—some of us like to eat our feelings, some of us prefer to have them massaged away by a bulky Salvadoran named Javier. So do unto yourself as you would do unto others, and trade those worries for a trip to Cupcakes "R" Us, or an hour of shoulder work from Javi. Yummy either way.

> **5 things I have stopped worrying about while eating a king-sized Snickers bar**
>
> Final exams
> Thunder
> Credit card debt
> Nuclear proliferation
> That rat I saw outside the deli where I bought the Snickers

How to stop being angry about something

Exhaling bitchily, shouting "Shut the fuck up!" every five minutes, and jabbing a broom through the hole in the fence that separates your yard from the neighbor's new pet rooster is one way to pass the time, but it's not a good long-term use of freakout funds. Trust me on this.

Instead, calm the fuck down by redirecting that time and energy into more PEACEFUL pursuits.

WORK IT OUT

I said I wouldn't make you get physical with your mental decluttering, but sometimes I fib, like the lady who waxed my bikini area for the first time ever and told me the worst part was over *and then she did the middle.*

But I digress.

Serotonin, known as "the happiness hormone," can be naturally boosted in many ways, including by exercise. But that doesn't have to mean dragging ass to the gym, *per se*. Sure, you can run out your rage on the treadmill or crunch your way to calm—if that works for you, so be it. Even I sometimes enjoy a low-impact stroll on the beach to clear my mind of rooster-cidal thoughts. Got a stairwell in your office? Walk up and down it until you no longer want to tear your boss a new asshole with his own tie pin. Empty lot down the street? Cartwheels! Empty lot down the street, under cover of night? NAKED CARTWHEELS.

PLOT YOUR REVENGE

Hopefully they won't revoke my guru card for this one, but let's just say you live downstairs from Carl and his all-night drug parties, and every morning your anger rises just as he and his crew finally drop off into a cracked-out slumber. Instead of seething into your dark roast, you might consider perking up by mentally cataloguing the ways in which you could repay your neighbors' kindness. You don't have to follow through—merely thinking about the mayhem you *could* visit upon your enemies is a terrific mood booster. (Though "accidentally" upending a bottle of clam juice into Carl's open car window on your way to work is fun too.)

5 forms of revenge that are fun to think about

Writing your enemy's phone number and a related "service" on the wall of a sketchy bar bathroom

Or, like, fifty sketchy bar bathrooms

Ordering a 4:00 a.m. wakeup call to your enemy's hotel room

Mailing your enemy a box of loose black pepper

Filling your enemy's pants pockets with gum right before they go into the wash

How to stop avoiding something

If anxiety sends you into overthinking, overwhelmed, overstimulation mode, then avoidance sends you in the exact opposite direction. Your worries have you paralyzed with inaction, indecision, and inability to deal. You may *think* you're saving freakout funds with all this inactivity, but you're actually wasting a lot of time that could otherwise be spent shoveling shit off your plate. It's the difference between napping as healthy self-care and napping as unhealthy coping mechanism. Let's not ruin napping for ourselves, okay?

Instead, try these ACTIVE alternatives on for size:

GET ALARMED

If you're putting something off — say, having "the talk" with your teenage son — use the alarm feature on your smartphone or watch to remind you about it ten times a day until you'd rather unroll a condom onto a banana than listen to that infernal jingle-jangle ONE MORE TIME. Even if you chicken out yet again, you'll have forced yourself to acknowledge the situation with every beep of your alarm, and that's half the battle.

(Actually, if you've been paying attention, it's one third of the battle. The middle third is *accepting* that you can't control a fifteen-year-old's libido, and the final third is *addressing* the part you can control — teaching safe sex — with prophylactics and phallic produce. You're welcome.)

PROPOSE A TRADE

If you're the ostriching type, I bet you're avoiding a few things at once. Oh, I'm right? Funny how that works. Well, just like focusing on one anxiety-inducing shitstorm at a time helps clear the deck of another set of worries (see: Choose it or lose it), you could make a deal with yourself that you only get to *avoid* one thing at a time. For example, if you're avoiding going to the doctor to get that suspicious mole checked out, you're not allowed to ALSO avoid balancing your checkbook.

And while you might be avoiding each of these activities because you additionally wish to avoid "getting bad news," I should point out that closing your eyes, plugging your ears, and singing "Nah nah nah nah" never stopped a hurricane from making landfall, and it's not going to halt the total shitstorm of skin cancer or bankruptcy. Confront the fear behind the worry now, so at least you have a *chance* to deal with it if it turns out to be warranted.

Is sleight of mind a little sneaky? Maybe. But you have to admit, it's hard to freak out while you're enjoying yourself — whether that's laughing at a silly movie, savoring a tasty treat, or focusing on getting every last drop of clam juice out of the bottle and absorbed deep into a Subaru's upholstery.

And if you ostriches took my advice and sprang into action, well, you may still be worrying a little as you sit in your dermatologist's waiting room, but you're also not avoiding it anymore. I call that a win.

Secret Option C

"Just fucking let it go" and "sleight of mind" are two excellent paths forward to a calmer, happier you. Highly recommended.

But depending on the person and worry and related shitstorm in question, these two methods alone are not always enough. I understand. And I'm not here to set you up for failure; if I wanted to do that, I would have called the book *How to Reason with a Toddler.*

As such, it's time for me to make a confession. **Despite its powerful cross-branding with my NotSorry Method from** *The Life-Changing Magic of Not Giving a Fuck* **and a very strong hashtag, the "NoWorries" Method may be a slight misnomer.**

No worries — like actually zero? Ever? That's probably not strictly possible. Sometimes your probometer is in the shop and your worries remain omnipresent and all-consuming. Sometimes you really just can't stop worrying or focus on other things.

It's okay, we can work with that.

Much like the "responsible procrastination" I detailed in *Get Your Shit Together,* or the "good selfish" discussed in *You Do You,* **there is such a thing as "useful worrying."**

You might engage in it in order to prevent the thing you're worried about from ever happening — as with a Category 1 Highly Unlikely Shitstorm that could be blown out to sea with a preemptive strike on your part.

Or, you might do some useful worrying to help yourself be in better shape when the shitstorm lands — as in the case of a Category 5 Inevitable. There's bound to be a lot less cleanup if you've adequately prepped the metaphorical house and grounds. (PS Have you made that dermatologist appointment yet?)

Wait, both of those sound like "dealing with it." Did you skip ahead?

Good on you for paying attention! But I really try not to skip ahead; it sets a bad example for my readers. No, what I'm about to teach you isn't quite "dealing with it," which we will cover in the aptly titled part III: Deal With It. This is sort of an in-between step.

Ladies and Gentlemen of the Worry, I give you...

Productive Helpful Effective Worrying (PHEW)

Up to this point, our goal has been to discard worries about shit you can't control, saving your time, energy, and money for dealing with the shit you can. We've been **CONSERVING freakout funds.**

That's one way to do it.

If you can't bring yourself to discard your worries altogether, another way to calm the fuck down is to **CONVERT those worries into productive, beneficial action — ensuring that any FFs you dole out in advance of a shitstorm are spent wisely.** They will (at least) help *prepare* you for surviving it; and (at best) help *prevent* it altogether.

That's what makes it PRODUCTIVE, HELPFUL, and EFFECTIVE worrying. The awesome acronym is just a side benefit. Here's how it plays out:

- Once a shitstorm has been classified and prioritized, the **NoWorries Method** dictates that you ask yourself *Can I control it?*

- If the answer is no, ideally you ACCEPT that you can't control it, and discard said worry. That's **Step 1: Calm the fuck down.**

- If the answer is yes, I can control it, then YAY! You may proceed directly to **Step 2: Deal with it,** organizing your response.

- However, if the answer is *No, I can't control it, BUT I ALSO CAN'T STOP WORRYING ABOUT IT OR DISTRACT MYSELF WITH OTHER THINGS!* then it's time to do some **Productive Helpful Effective Worrying.**

As an example, let's examine a perpetually outlying shitstorm offered by an anxious parent in my Twitter feed:

- **What if I fuck up my kids and turn them into bad people?**

This is a big, complex worry that causes many parents low-level anxiety every day, plus occasional bouts of hard-core freaking out.

Challenge accepted!

First, I absolutely understand why lots of them might not be able to "just fucking let it go." And I understand that it might be hard to employ sleight of mind and focus on other things while parenting. In fact, maybe you shouldn't get too distracted. Especially at the playground. Accidents happen.

But I humbly suggest that what you *could* do if you are constantly worried about fucking up your kids and turning them into bad people — and you are unable to let that worry go — is to spend your time, energy, and money on being the best parent you, personally, can be.

You don't have complete control over whether your kid turns out to be a bad person. At some point, that's on them. **But you can indulge your worries and *at the same time* contribute to the cause** by engaging in child-rearing tactics that are objectively proven to result in positives — such as reading to your kids, telling your kids you love them and are proud of them, and teaching them to say please and thank you and to not kick sand on me at the beach.

At least if you're taking these actions — **actions that are not shifting your focus via sleight of mind, but rather are *directly related* to the worry at hand** — you may still be yanking your metaphorical yarn, but you also know you're doing what you can to help your kids become good people.

That's PHEW in a nutshell. Not the worst advice you've ever received, if I do say so myself. (It's also not the first time I've given it here in this very book. Remember Really Cool Hat Guy? That was PHEW—you just didn't know it yet.)

You can't stop worrying? Fine. Worry away! But make it count for something.

Sending a shitstorm out to sea

As someone who once sat glued to the Weather Channel for ten days as two Category 5 hurricanes charted a collision course with my home on a fragile Caribbean peninsula, I know there is no greater relief than watching a seemingly inevitable monster storm veer away at the eleventh hour.

But of course, those near misses were due to sheer luck. (As Puerto Ricans know all too well, both Mother Nature and a certain world leader are capricious when it comes to visiting chaos and destruction upon a people.)

When it's a *shitstorm* on the radar, however—and a low-probability one at that—**you may be able to engineer a downgrade.** Sometimes you can gin that probometer readout from a 2 or 1 down to a harmless little tropical shitclone that potters off the grid before you can say "I presided over and directly contributed to the worst humanitarian crisis America has seen since the Civil War."

There are two different ways to prevent an already unlikely shitstorm from making landfall:

1. Take action (PHEW)
2. Do nothing (Counterintuitive, I know. Bear with me.)

Each has its place; deciding to implement one or the other is simply a matter of recognizing what you can control, and then acting (or not acting) accordingly. For example:

- **What if I spend thousands of dollars to paint my house and on a large scale the color turns out to be ugly?**

  Action you could take: They have apps and online simulators for this. Do your research. (Same goes for drastic haircuts, BTW.)
  Outcome: No surprises.

- **What if my wife doesn't like the gift I bought her for our 25th anniversary?**

  Action you could take: You're so sweet! Ask your wife's most trusted friend to help you shop, or to slyly solicit ideas from her BFF over coffee. Also: DIAMONDS.
  Outcome: Happy wife, happy life.

- **What if I get seasick on my first-ever boat ride, which also happens to be my best chance to impress a client on his private catamaran?**

Action you could take: Dramamine, for the win.
Outcome: Your cookies remain untossed.

In each of the above scenarios, the total shitstorm is unlikely to evolve, but if you know you're going to be worrying about it anyway, you can take action to prevent it.

If you like that shade of blue on a small scale, chances are you'll like it at split-level size, but it pays to make sure beforehand. If you've been married for twenty-five years, you probably have a pretty good sense of your beloved's taste, but calling for reinforcements can only improve your chances of a tearful "Oh my God, how did you know?!?" (Maybe improve your chances of a little something else, too, *if* you know what I mean…) And not everyone experiences motion sickness, but there's no point in finding out you're susceptible the moment you're attempting to close a deal. "Barfs on clients" doesn't look good on your LinkedIn profile.

Sure, these happen to be somewhat low-level problems with fairly easy, self-evident solutions, but that's what made them unlikely to begin with. If you're the kind of person who worries about unlikely shit happening, you just gained the perspective to wipe a few Category 1s and 2s off the screen before breakfast. Not too shabby.

Your other option to stave off a shitstorm is to do nothing at all.

Yes, I know, I've previously advocated for taking action in order to prevent a freakout, but now we're talking about *the problem itself,* not *your reaction to it.* If you can blow the shitstorm out to sea by taking ZERO action, the freakout is rendered moot anyway.

Like, let's say you're hella concerned about the prospect of an unwanted pregnancy. If you use birth control regularly (and properly), then *What if I get pregnant?* should already be a Cat. 1 Highly Unlikely — but if you really can't afford any room for error, I know just the thing to nip that fetus in the bud.

Abstinence! I'm talking about abstinence, guys. Jesus.

Hey, if you care as much about sex as I do about skiing, then doing nothing totally works. Groan away, but it's true, isn't it? In fact, there's really no limit to the things you could *never* do if you *never* want to risk a potential bad outcome — **as long as whatever you're giving up is worth the sacrifice.**

For example:

You could never go canoeing so that you never flip over in a canoe and drown. There are other ways to transport oneself across water. Like bridges.

You could never handle fireworks, so that you never get into a freak Roman candle accident. You know what they say: it's all fun and games until someone has to be fitted for a glass eye.

Or you could never agree to retrieve the sacred sivalinga stone for the villagers of Mayapore and therefore never be forced to drink the blood of Kali and almost die at the hands of a prepubescent maharaja in a faraway temple of doom. Easy-peasy.

Are you sensing a little sarcasm here? Good. You sense correctly. Because what's not useful is *never doing something* because you're afraid of an outcome so unlikely in its own right that you'd actually be doing yourself a bigger disservice by avoiding the original thing entirely.

Or to put it another way, **being crippled by anxiety is no way to live.**

Houston, we have an irrational fear

I'd like to treat you to a bonus what-if scenario that's near and dear to my own heart, and that **might give you a new way of looking at something you may have long considered an insurmountable problem.** Or this could be the point in the book where you snort derisively, proclaim me a fucking idiot, and go on your merry way. It's your world, squirrel.

For the sake of argument, let's imagine that you're traveling from New York to New Mexico, and you're worried that this Delta Death Blimp is destined to go down over the Great Lakes and take you and 114 other easy marks along with it.

The first step toward staving off a freakout in Terminal A is to categorize the potential shitstorm in question (dying in a plane crash), and **acknowledge that it's not *probable.***

To wit: the odds of dying in a plane crash are one in eleven million, which makes it less likely than being killed by a shark (one in eight million), dying on a cruise ship (one in 6.25 million), or getting hit by lightning (one in twelve thousand).

You are dealing with a Category 1 Highly Unlikely here. No two ways about it. Furthermore, even if your 747 *is* destined to fall out of the sky like a drone operated by your drunk uncle Ronnie at a Freemasons' picnic, **what the fuck are you going to do about it?***

Unless you plan to abandon your current career to spend a couple of years in flight school and become a pilot, which you would have to overcome your fear of flying to do in the first place, **you cannot control the situation. It is 100 percent out of your hands.**

Which means what?

---

* At this time, I would like to apologize to anyone who bought this book at the airport for a bit of light travel reading.

THAT'S RIGHT. It's a waste of time and energy to worry about it.

If you still want to play devil's advocate, I suppose you could also control the situation by never flying anywhere, ever — but then you should stop driving, riding, sailing, walking, or roller-blading anywhere too, because the probability of death goes way up the closer to Earth you travel.

Let's stop talking about it.

The thing is, I know that the irrational fear of flying (or irrational fear of anything, for that matter) is very upsetting. I myself am terrified of air travel for all kinds of reasons that, when examined in the weak glow of the overhead light, do not hold up.

So when I'm settled into seat 5A staring down the barrel of a cross-country hop to give a lecture at Marriott Corporate on getting your shit together, I counter this pernicious what-if with a big ol' dose of *Is there one single goddamn thing you can do to prevent this plane from exploding, falling apart, or dropping out of the sky? No? Then calm the fuck down and worry about something you* can *control, like writing out your speech all professional-like on some index cards and then not spilling your miniature vodka tonic on them.*

I also treat this particular case of the what-ifs with .25 milli-grams of Xanax, but that's beside the point. I didn't even have a Xanax prescription for the first thirty years of my life and I still got on planes when I was feeling wicked anxious because it's just not logical or rational to avoid them for eternity—and, as mentioned previously, I am a very logical and rational person.

Most of the time.

Hi, I'm Sarah and I have a mental illness (More than one, actually!)

As you may have gleaned, I'm a proponent of better living not only through logic and reason and emotional puppy crating, but also through pharmaceuticals. In addition to employing nonchemical techniques like deep breathing and walking on the beach and balancing pineapples on my head, I take different daily and situational prescription medications to keep a lid on my anxiety and keep panic attacks at bay. And I TAKE THEM BECAUSE THEY WORK. Pills aren't for everyone, of course, and neither is meditation or electroconvulsive therapy. But I want to talk about this stuff to do my small part to help eradicate the stigma surrounding mental health issues and getting treatment for them. Mental illness is a disease like any other and if *that's* your underlying problem, you don't deserve to be shamed for or feel shame about it.

There, I said it. Now back to our regularly scheduled menu of absurd hypotheticals, dirty jokes, and meteorological metaphors.

The calm before the shitstorm

At this point in our journey—a word I use with the utmost sarcasm—I hope you're feeling really good about your prospects for calming the fuck down.

- You've been armed with the knowledge and tools to **prioritize.**
- You understand the concept of **control** and **what it means to accept that which you cannot.**
- And I've presented you with many techniques for **discarding, distracting yourself from, or converting your what-ifs and worries** like a boss—and **steering clear of freakouts** along the way.

As such, now is the time on *Sprockets* when we put everything you've learned into action.*

To show you how it's done, I'm returning to the what-ifs from the list I made at the beginning of part II. I already gave you my thought process for categorizing each of those potential shitstorms. That's where I **ACKNOWLEDGED** them. Here, I'll go

---

* To those of you who got that reference, congrats on being at least forty.

further, asking myself which parts of these potential shitstorms I can control — and then **ACCEPTING** the answers, aka the reality of my situation(s).

We'll start at the bottom of the Shitstorm Scale with my Category 1s & 2s, and work our way up.

10 WHAT-IFS I MAY OR MAY NOT NEED TO WORRY ABOUT: CAN I CONTROL THEM?

CATEGORY 1 — HIGHLY UNLIKELY

What if...

- **More tarantulas appear in my house**

Can I control it? Nope. On the sliding scale of control, this is an "out of my hands" for the ages. When it comes to worrying about tarantulas, I'm going to just fucking let it go. (And if Lucky comes back a third time, I think he's officially our pet.)

- **I order a different pizza than usual and it isn't very good**

Can I control it? Yes, but that's exactly why it's highly unlikely to happen in the first place. Every practice test has a trick question.

- **My editor hates this chapter**

Can I control it? I can definitely heavily influence this outcome by not sending Mike a piece of shit, but then again, his opinion is his alone. However, one's thing's for sure: if I'm sitting here obsessing over what he might think about something I sent him, then I'm taking time away from finishing the rest of the book — arguably a worse outcome, since I'm on a bit of a deadline here. So I've elected to press SEND and **convert those worries** (productively, helpfully, and effectively) into "writing more chapters." Then on the off chance that he *does* hate this one, I'll spend my FFs ordering a perfectly topped large pizza, calming the fuck down, and dealing with the revisions.

CATEGORY 2 — POSSIBLE BUT NOT LIKELY

What if...

- **My house key gets stuck in the door**

Can I control it? Since I don't know why it happened the first time, there's nothing I can do to ensure it doesn't happen again — except stop locking the house altogether, which invites a shitstorm of a different stripe. Nope, can't control it, so I'll discard that worry and save my freakout funds for conducting a little light B&E if necessary.

- **A palm tree falls on my roof**

Can I control it? Nope. (Technically, I could spend some time, energy, and money on Productive Helpful Effective Worrying and have the two trees within spitting distance cut down before they can fuck with us, but they grow out of the neighbor's yard and I don't think she'd appreciate it; plus then I wouldn't get to look at them every day while I bob in my pool.) The freakout funds remains untouched... for now.

- **I get into a car accident on the winding mountain road to the airport**

Can I control it? This is a "contribute to the cause" situation. The reasons for the difference between the amount of freakout funding I give to speaking gigs (a lot) vs. the Return of Lucky (none) vs. airport transport (some) are simple: My relative preparedness for a speech, I can heavily influence. But I can't do anything about keeping the tarantula out. Spiders gonna spider. Whereas on the airport road, although I'm not driving the car myself and *directly* influencing the ride, I can control *whether* we only book flights that have us traveling that stretch during daylight hours, and I'm not shy about asking the driver to slow down or pull over if it starts pouring rain. Control what you can, accept what you can't, and wear your seat belt.

- **I show up for a speaking gig and totally bomb**

Can I control it? Again, yes, but the way to control this outcome is *not* by worrying about failing. It's by spending my time and energy preparing a great talk and rehearsing the shit out of it. PHEW. So productive! So helpful! So effective! (And sure, there's a first time for everything, but if I worried about that I would have used up all my freakout funds on *What if aliens invade Earth and make us their space bitches?* a long time ago.)

Et voilà! With seven unlikely what-ifs on my radar, I've **CONSERVED** freakout funds by discarding my worries about four of them (tarantulas, bad pizza, stuck keys, fallen palms), and **CONVERTED** funds via Productive Helpful Effective Worrying for three more (speaking gig fails, seat belts, subsequent chapters).

I've still got plenty of FFs in reserve for total shitstorms, if (Categories 3 and 4) and when (Category 5) they occur.

CATEGORY 3 — LIKELY

What if...

- **I ruin my favorite pineapple-print shorts by sitting in something nasty**

Can I control it? Eh. I can heavily influence this outcome by watching where I sit, but I don't want that to be my full-time job, so I've decided to let this one go. Thus far, club soda and dish soap have staved off ruination, but one day it's likely that the shorts will be unsalvageable, at which time I will spend $16 in freakout funds to get another pair from Target and restart the clock. Discard that worry for now.

CATEGORY 4 — HIGHLY LIKELY

What if…

- **It rains on my day off that I wanted to spend at the beach**

Can I control it? That's a big "no" to the weather itself and "barely" in terms of predicting it. Weather apps might as well be made of old soup cans and string for all the good they do me here. This is a perfect example of a shitstorm that — despite its high level of probability — is pointless to worry about. (In this case, a nice tall piña colada does wonders for my attitude.)

CATEGORY 5 — INEVITABLE

What if…

- **My cats die**

Can I control it? Nope. That's the thing about "average lifespans." Should I spend FFs worrying about it? Hell nope! I've suffered through the deaths of a couple of pets in my time, and it's horrible. When it happens again, I'll be really sad, but I'll deal with it then. What I'm not going to do is preemptively freak out and stop surrounding myself with feline friends just because one day I'm going to have to decide where to display their ashes or whether to have them stuffed and mounted above the dining table over my husband's strenuous objections.

Now you try, with that same list of what-ifs you made on page 77 and that you already sorted by category. Use these questions as your guide:

- Can I **control** it?

- If not, can I **accept** that reality, **stop worrying about it**, and **conserve** freakout funds?

- If I can't stop worrying about it, can I **convert** freakout funds to **productive, helpful, effective worrying** that will prevent or mitigate it?

10 WHAT-IFS I MAY OR MAY NOT NEED TO WORRY ABOUT: CAN I CONTROL THEM?

_____

Category: _____

Can I control it? [Y] [N]

_____

Category: _____

Can I control it? [Y] [N]

_____

Category: _____

Can I control it? [Y] [N]

_____

Category: _____

Can I control it? [Y] [N]

_____

Category: _____

Can I control it? [Y] [N]

_____

Category: _____

Can I control it? [Y] [N]

_____

Category: _____

Can I control it? [Y] [N]

_____

Category: _____

Can I control it? [Y] [N]

_____

Category: _____

Can I control it? [Y] [N]

_____

Category: _____

Can I control it? [Y] [N]

Are you feeling a little more — dare I say it — in control? I hope so, and I hope asking the One Question to Rule Them All becomes a vibrant element of your daily process.

It certainly has for me; I estimate that I'm 75 percent less basket case-y as a result.

In fact, lately it's been especially helpful being able to categorize my what-ifs and let go of stuff I can't control. Have you been watching CNN? I'm surprised the chyron below Jake Tapper's skeptical mug doesn't just run "THIS SHIT IS BANANAS" on infinite loop. When nearly every hour of every day brings to light some further debasement America and/or the rest of the world has endured at the tiny paws of a D-list wannabe Mafioso — well, it's useful to have some defense mechanisms firmly in place.

I read the news today, oh boy

It did not take a master's in guruing to discern that as of the time of this writing, people around the world are more in need than ever of calming the fuck down.

The United States of America, as mentioned, is a total shitshow. The president is an unhinged narcissist, the ruling political party is composed largely of simpering cowards, and affordable health care is nothing more than a collective hallucination — treatment for which is not covered by your insurance company.

England and the rest of the United [for now] Kingdom: not doing so hot either. Perhaps you've noticed? In fact, if you watch the news, or even just scroll through Twitter, it seems like every continent is seeing fascism, xenophobia, and sea levels on the rise — or icebergs, honeybees, and civil liberties on the decline.

Ugh.

I don't know if there's actually *more* war, pestilence, extreme weather, or dismaying cultural regression going on than ever before, but I do know we're more *aware of it,* because technology has seen to it that humans can't go a millisecond without finding out about the latest school shooting, terror attack, election meddling, or rendezvous between evil dictators hell-bent on destroying Western civilization.

Double UGH.

It's a problem, and one I hope this book will help you address in some small but significant way, she writes, as women's right to bodily autonomy hangs perpetually in the balance.

ROE V. UGHHH.

What to do? Well, because I still believe in the benefits of an informed/enraged citizenry, I'm afraid I cannot personally advocate for Total Ostrich Mode, aka "not consuming the news at all." But a few minor bouts of ostriching in service to shit you can't control? I'll allow it. Go on, get that face in the pillows and that ass in the air!

As to anger, you're entitled. Letting loose a full-throated howl *while* your face is in the pillows can be satisfying. You know, if the mood strikes. And if you can channel your anger into something productive, so much the better — like, after hurling every glass container in your home against a wall as though it were an old white man trying to steal your children's future, you could take out the recycling. Smash the patriarchy, save the planet.

When you're done — and apart from just hoping things will improve or that you can primal scream them into submission — **there are other ways to counteract the feelings of helplessness** you might have when being bombarded daily with the worst the media has to offer. Rather than scrolling through your newsfeeds each night before bed and giving yourself teeth-falling-out dreams, perhaps you could try one of the following **calming, control-regaining techniques?**

They work for me, and I'm about as despondent over crumbling democracy and devastating climate crisis as it gets!

5 TIPS FOR CALMING THE FUCK DOWN ABOUT THE WORLD FALLING APART

LIMIT YOUR EXPOSURE

An informed citizen doesn't have to be gathering information over breakfast, on the toilet, astride an exercise bike, during their commute, AND right before going to sleep (or trying to go to sleep, anyway). A once-per-day news dump should be sufficient to keep you in the know without also keeping your blood pressure higher than Snoop Dogg.

BALANCING ACT

If you can't dodge the twenty-four-hour news cycle, for every @WashingtonPost you follow, add a palliative account to the mix. I recommend @PepitoTheCat, which is just time-stamped black-and-white footage of some cat in France coming and going through his cat door, accompanied by the captions "Pépito is out" or "Pépito is back home." I like to scroll through Pépito's feed before bed. It's like counting sheep, but instead you're counting the same French cat over and over again. *Trés* relaxing.

BONE UP

It may seem counterintuitive, but doing a deep dive into whatever single current event is giving you the biggest case of the what-ifs can help you vanquish some of your more paranoid fantasies. For example, researching how the "nuclear football" actually works and learning that a certain feeble-minded president would have to memorize certain information in order to launch an attack may have done wonders for a certain someone's ability to stop worrying [quite so much] about the prospect of this particular mushroom shitcloud sprouting anytime soon.

TAKE A MEMO

Drafting an angry letter — to a global leader, a local representa-tive, or, say, morally repugnant NRA spokeswoman Dana

Loesch — can really get the mad out of you. Journaling is scientifically proven to help calm you down by moving all those burning, churning thoughts out of your head and onto the page. And you don't even have to send your angry missive to reap the in-the-moment benefit, but for the cost of a stamp it might be nice to know it'll reach its intended target. Or at least clutter their inbox, which in my opinion is a fate worse than death.

DO GOOD

When I'm feeling powerless about the state of the world, one thing that brings me comfort is donating to a cause — be it a natural disaster relief fund, a local charity, or just a single person who needs a hand. Is this my economic privilege talking? Sure, but if spending my freakout funds this way makes me feel better *and* helps someone less fortunate, all I see is a two-for-one special on good deeds. And "giving" needn't require a cash outlay — you have other FFs at your disposal. Time and energy spent calling your reps to protest inhumane immigration practices, volunteering at Planned Parenthood, or mocking up some zesty protest signs and taking a brisk walk around your nearest city center will help you sleep better in more ways than one.

Now if you'll excuse me, while my husband is watching the orange howler monkey's latest antics on MSNBC, I have a French cat's whereabouts to monitor.

(Pépito is out.)

Stirring the shit

Okay, folks. We are neck-deep in part II. I trust you're starting to see that, **logically and rationally, much of the shit you worry about is unlikely to happen**—and that you can do enough PHEW-ing to ensure that even the likely stuff can be made less terrible with some effort on your part. Just don't get cocky.

I would be remiss if I didn't warn you that **it is possible to trick yourself into *thinking* you're PHEW-ing, when what you are really doing is WILLING A SHITSTORM INTO EXISTENCE.**

In psychological terms, **"catastrophizing"** is the belief that a situation is worse than it actually is. And I promised I wouldn't argue with you about how hard things suck for you right now. I fucking hate it when people do that. But **if you *do* happen to be catastrophizing, you may also be *creating your own catastrophe***—something I can and will caution you against.

That's right: you have the ability to send a shitstorm out to sea, but also to conjure a Category 5 out of thin air.

For example, if your friend Andy hasn't gotten back to you about you taking his extra ticket for the Cubs game tomorrow night and you're paranoid that he's mad at you even though he hasn't said anything specific, you might text him to be like, "Hey dude, are you pissed because I wrote your email address on that

Church of Scientology sign-up sheet? Sorry, they surrounded me when I was leaving the gym and I panicked. My bad."

And maybe he wasn't mad at you (just busy getting off the Church of Scientology mailing list). BUT NOW HE IS.

If you'd stopped to study all available data you would have realized there was no way Andy could have known you were the clipboard culprit. If you hadn't panic-texted, he never would have put two and Xenu together and you'd be slammin' deep dish in the box seats — no harm, no foul.

Instead, you overthought it and you're watching the game on TV with your good friend Papa John.

Other times, when a shitstorm is already tracking as "inevitable," your actions may significantly hasten its arrival and amplify its effects.

Historically, this has been a bit of a problem for yours truly. On the one hand, and as I wrote about in *You Do You*, my natural tendency toward anxiety can in some ways be a good thing. It helps me plan ahead, because I can envision the perils and consequences of not doing so. It helps me be prepared, be on time, and generally stay on top of my shit.

But every once in a while, the anxiety, and the overthinking it enables, knocks over a domino that might never have fallen on its own.

And then I'm left picking up the whole damn pile.

That was not a chill pill

It was finals week during my junior year of college. I had exams to study for and papers to write, and both time and energy were running low. I'd done all the research for my last remaining essay, but it was already early evening the night before it was due. My late-nineties desktop computer sat there judging me like Judy.

I was mentally and physically exhausted, at the end of an already frayed rope. I knew I didn't have the juice — let alone the hours on the clock — to pull this one out. But as a classic over-achiever and rule-follower, the prospect of not handing in an assignment on time was simply off the table. I couldn't fail to show up at my professor's office at 9:00 a.m. with dot-matrix printout in hand, and I for damn sure couldn't beg for an extension on a *final paper*. That would be madness!

Speaking of which, I had started to go a little nutso myself worrying about what would happen when I blew this assignment — and in the throes of the ensuing freakout I made a Very Bad Decision in service to what I *thought* was Productive Helpful Effective Worrying.

Can't stay awake for the limited number of hours left in which to craft a piece of writing that will account for 25 percent of your final grade in a Harvard undergraduate seminar?

Accept two mystery pills from a friend who tells you "This will keep you up and help you focus!"

NARRATOR: It kept her up. It did not help her focus.

By dawn I was thoroughly cracked out, defeated, and dehydrated from an hour or so of inconsolable sobbing triggered by the realization that I was *definitely* not going to finish this paper on time. Since swallowing the mystery pills I'd spent ten hours growing increasingly frantic, my heart thumping in my chest, fingers shaking over my keyboard, and pacing my dorm room like an extra in *Orange Is the New Black*.

Now it was time to swallow something else: my pride.

Still huffing and snuffling, I pecked out an email to my professor. Rather than compound my sins by concocting a dead grandmother or severe tendinitis, I decided to tell her the truth — that I had backed myself into a corner time-wise and attempted to rectify my [first] mistake with an influx of energy-by-what-was-probably-Adderall. I was sorry and ashamed and had generated four pages of gobbledygook instead of fifteen pages of cogent argument. I needed an extra day.

Then I collapsed onto my futon and waited for the other Doc Marten to fall. (As mentioned, it was the late nineties.)

My professor didn't curse or rage or threaten to have me expelled. She was matter-of-fact about the whole situation. She granted me the bonus time and said whatever grade I received on merit would have to be taken down a point for lateness.

Well, that was ... easier than I thought it would be.

I still had to deal with the original task, sure. But in the meantime, I'd had to deal with the total shitstorm I'd summoned by freaking out about the original task and making a Very Bad Decision fueled by anxiety. Had I been able to calm the fuck down in the first place, I might have missed my deadline, but I would have asked for the extension up front; gotten a good night's sleep; spent the following day writing my paper with a fresh brain; and avoided the ten-hour interlude of weeping, shaking, and pacing.

Also: I would have avoided emailing my professor at six in the morning to tell her I TOOK SPEED. So there's that.

I love it when a plan comes together

Before we round the corner to part III: Deal With It, I feel a pressing urge to drive home the power of all of the tips and techniques from part II. What can I say? Sometimes I just can't stop guruing.

In the next few pages, I'm going to take a sample what-if and help you calm the fuck down about it. We will:

- Assign a category and status to this potential shitstorm
- Determine what (if any) control you might have over the outcome
- Accept the reality of the situation
- Discard worries stemming from the parts you can't control

- Spend your freakout funds wisely to prevent, prepare for, or mitigate the results of the rest.

I'll even throw in a preview of dealing with it, because I'm a full-service anti-guru and I respect a seamless transition.

Categorizin' cousins

Let's say, hypothetically, you have two cousins named Renée and Julie. Recently Renée posted something nasty on Facebook that was oblique-yet-clearly-aimed-at-Julie, and now the two of them are about to cross paths…at your wedding.

Do you feel a freakout coming on?

Assuming for the sake of our hypothetical that the answer is yes (or that you can imagine how it would be a yes for some people, given that weddings are traditionally known to be intrafamilial hotbeds of stress and strife), you have a decision to make.

You could spend time and energy worrying about your cousins getting into a parking lot fistfight during the reception, working yourself into a double-whammy Anxious/Angry Freakout Face — but that's neither going to prevent it from happening nor help you deal with it.

Instead, let's **activate your inner whetherperson and assemble all the available data.** Such as:

- What's Renée and Julie's history?
- Has this kind of thing happened before?
- How well do they hold their liquor?

Asking logical, rational questions like these will help you determine whether it's HIGHLY UNLIKELY, POSSIBLE BUT NOT LIKELY, LIKELY, HIGHLY LIKELY, or INEVITABLE that these bitches are getting ready to rumble.

And who knows? Maybe they'll be so inspired by your vows that they will "vow" to stop being so nasty to each other. Maybe they'll hug and make up in the photo booth, before the pigs in blankets hit the buffet. Maybe at least one of them will take the high road as her wedding gift to you.

I certainly don't know, because I don't know them — but *you* do. **Check your probometer** and make a reasonable guess as to which category this potential shitstorm falls under. Then earmark your freakout funds accordingly.

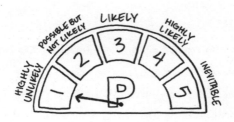

SCENARIO 1

Trolling each other online is Renée and Julie's standard MO and so far, it hasn't resulted in a parking lot fistfight. They tend to circle each other like wary cats, bond over their shared passion for twerking to Nicki Minaj, and then all is forgiven over the third SoCo-and-lime shot of the night.

Probometer Readout: Cat. 1 / 2 — Highly Unlikely or Possible But Not Likely

- Worrying about something that's unlikely to happen is a risky use of valuable freakout funds. You know this. If the storm never comes to pass, you've wasted time, energy, and/or money; and if it *does* happen, you'll be forced to pay double — having freaked out about it then + having to deal with it now. **Conclusion:** Your FFs are better reserved for other potential wedding day snafus. We all know your friend Travis is a loose cannon.

SCENARIO 2

Your cousins always had a complicated relationship, but it's gotten more volatile in the last year, ever since Julie dropped Renée from their *RuPaul's Drag Race* recap WhatsApp group. Ice cold. Of course you can never be 100 percent sure what she's thinking, but Renée is not one to let sleeping drag queens lie.

Probometer Readout: Cat. 3 / 4 — Likely or Highly Likely

- If you're that much more convinced the shitstorm is coming, you also have that much of a better idea about when it will land. **If it's a 3 or 4, you should do a status check.** Are we talking merely OUTLYING (it's a few weeks before the wedding) or IMMINENT (it's the morning of the wedding)? The status informs **how *soon* you need to spend your freakout funds on prevention or mitigation.**

- But before you dole out any FFs to a Category 3 or 4 shitstorm, you should ask yourself *Can I control it?*

If the answer is "Nope, out of my hands" (e.g., your cousins have never listened to you a day in their lives; why would they start now?), then discard that worry like Travis will undoubtedly discard his bow tie when the first bars of "Hot in Herre" infiltrate the dance floor. Don't waste time, energy, and/or money *freaking out about it.* Consequently, if/when the girls do decide to take out their earrings and their aggression, you'll have that time, energy, and/or money to spend *dealing with it.*

(Still feeling anxious? Try a little sleight of mind. I hear calligraphy is relaxing, and if you start practicing now, maybe you can save some money on your invites.)

If the answer is a hearty *Yes, I can control or heavily influence this outcome!* (e.g., you believe your cousins will respond well to the threat of being cut off from the Southern Comfort if they misbehave), then by all means, whip out your worry wallet and peel off a thoughtfully composed email to Renée and Julie warning them that wedding day shenanigans will result in them being *personae non gratae* at the open bar. That's **Productive Helpful Effective Worrying** in action. Phew.

SCENARIO 3

Renée and Julie came to blows at your brother's state championship football game three years ago and dragged each other into the pond at their own mother's seventieth-birthday party. There is no reason to believe your wedding will count as sacred ground. These broads are out for blood. Their husbands are selling tickets and taking bets. The forecast is clear. It is ON.*

> *Probometer Readout: Cat. 5 — Inevitable*
>
> - I understand why you'd worry about something like this, which you believe is inevitable — it's human nature, and it's also YOUR FUCKING WEDDING DAY. On the other hand, **if it's inevitable and you can't control it,** perhaps you could accept that and let go of your worries unless/until you absolutely *must* spend some freakout funds dealing with the fallout?

---

* This is assuming you didn't disinvite them already, which would count as PHEW to the MAX but also leave me unable to follow this hypothetical to its messiest conclusion, and that's no fun.

- Furthermore, if you believe a conflagration of cousins is past the point of being staved off by PHEW on your part—then I'd suggest a big, fat **"Just fucking let it go."** You're about to embark on one of the most momentous occasions of your life. And whether it's in three months' or three hours' time, you do not need this shit.

- **ACKNOWLEDGE** that no matter what you do, your flesh and blood are gearing up for Parking Lot Grudge Match 3; **ACCEPT the reality;** and **ADDRESS it** when and only when it becomes a textbook total shitstorm.

  Do NOT spend freakout funds now. You're going to need that time, energy, and money when the total shitstorm makes landfall—time to collect yourself in the ladies' room; energy to kick some ass of your own; and money to post Julie's bail. Renée started it. Let her rot.

  But DO put fifty bucks on Julie. She spent the last six months taking jujitsu, which Renée would know if she weren't such a self-absorbed cunt.

Aaaaand that's a wrap on part II!

Or, well, not quite. There's a smidge more overly reductive yet extremely helpful content left to be had, and if you're a seasoned NFGG reader, you know what's coming…

OH YEAH, IT'S FLOWCHART TIME.

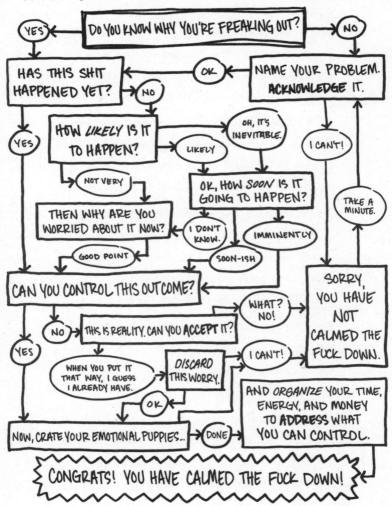

DEAL WITH IT:

Address what you *can* control

Hey, hey, hey, look at you! You made it to part III, where all of your rigorous training in calming the fuck down will be put to the ultimate test: **dealing with the shit you're worried about.**

And for the purposes of this section, we're going to assume this is **Shit That Has Already Happened.** Congrats, you're really moving up in the world.

Thus far, we've **dissected freaking out**—making you more aware of the symptoms and consequences of doing so. We've **wrestled with worrying**—not doing it with regard to things you can't control, and/or doing it more effectively. Those are the initial steps toward both **combating existential anxiety** and **surviving any shitstorm** that well and truly comes to pass.

You've already done a shit-ton of **mental decluttering, Step 1: Discarding.** You've rid yourself of so many unproductive worries that you should have a healthy supply of freakout funds left to move on to **Step 2: Organizing**—aka dealing with whatever's **left, now or in the future.**

Mental decluttering is like hanging up on telemarketers; learn it once and it's a skill that sticks with you for life.

Now it's time to introduce my **Three Principles of Dealing With It**—developed to help you and the 75 percent of people who responded to my survey by saying **they wish they had better coping mechanisms for when shit happens.**

Baby, I've got the only three you'll ever need.

I'll also help you identify your **RIOs (realistic ideal out-**

comes). These ensure that you don't waste time, energy, money, or goodwill dealing yourself down a rabbit hole of dubious destination.

Prescriptive pragmatism: learn it, live it.

Finally, we'll put it all into practice. The last section of part III functions like a catalogue of terror. In it, **I'll take you through a bunch of total shitstorm scenarios to illustrate how a logical, rational mind-set can help you deal with them.** We'll cover work mishaps, family feuds, missed opportunities, natural disasters, broken limbs, broken hearts, and broken dreams.

It'll be a hoot, I promise.

Of course, no single book or catalogue of terror can prepare you for each and every potential trauma life has to offer. But just like *Get Your Shit Together* offered a simple toolkit for proactively setting goals and achieving them, *Calm the Fuck Down* gives you the tools to **productively *react to* all the shit you didn't want and didn't choose** but that happened to you anyway because life isn't fair.

You just have to **ACKNOWLEDGE, ACCEPT,** and **ADDRESS** it.

If I have anything to say about it, by the time you turn the final page of part III you will be fully equipped to do just that.

Deal me in

"Dealing with it" encompasses a range of actions taken — and outcomes achieved — in response to shit happening.

At the top of the outcomes scale you've got the **FULL FIX**. Like, you left your iPhone X on the city bus, but realized it just in time to take off running like a bipedal cocker spaniel until a divinely placed red light allowed you time to catch up to the bus, rap on the door, indicate "I left my cell phone!" and reclaim your property.

Done. Like it never happened.

Below that, there are **SALVAGE JOBS**. You left your iPhone X on the bus and you didn't get it back, so you had to buy a new one. You dealt with it, but you spent a lot of freakout funds on that mistake. No Chinese takeout for you for the next two years, give or take.

Or maybe you can't afford a new iPhone X right now, so you curse your carelessness, learn a lesson, get a refurbished 5se off eBay, and go on with your life.* If you can't afford a replacement smartphone at all, you pick up a cheapie burner at Radio Shack that doesn't connect to the cloud and spend the next week asking

---

* I've been rocking a 5se since 2016. No complaints.

all your Facebook friends to resend you their contact info via smoke signal.

More FFs withdrawn, plus a smidgen of goodwill, but at least you're back in the game.

Below that, you've got **BASIC SURVIVAL.** You're between jobs and on a strict budget. You can't afford a new phone of any sort. You're anxious about missing a callback for an interview and angry that you put yourself in this position, but now that you've read this book, you're able to practice some sleight of mind and pull yourself together. **Focus, peace out, act up. You know the drill.**

Instead of letting this costly error further erode your fragile state of both mind and finances, you find a workaround, perhaps making a few withdrawals from the Fourth Fund (which is topped up, since you haven't been freaking the fuck out all the time lately like Sherry). Maybe you ask a friend or relative if they have a spare old phone lying around that they could activate for you. Definitely reach out to prospective employers to let them know you're temporarily without access to the number on your résumé and request that they make contact by email if they have news for you. You could start a GoFundMe page. Or sell your used panties on Craigslist. It's honest work.

Of course, a lost phone is just one example out of a million possibilities of shit happening that you then have to deal with. It may not apply to you (in fact, if you've read *Get Your Shit Together,* I hope you've been conditioned to never lose your phone under any circumstances).

Or maybe you could never afford an iPhone X in the first place, or you think I'm being cavalier in the face of something that, for you, would be a Really Fucking Big Problem that's Not So Easy to Solve. I understand; everyone's situation is different and their resource levels vary. Maybe no matter how much you want to, you can't run after that bus because you're still recovering from hip surgery.

I'm sorry about that. Get well soon.

My point is, this or any of the 999,999 thousand examples I could give totally sucks — yes indeedy — but there ARE ways to deal with it that don't involve purchasing a replacement iPhone X and that *also* don't involve crying into your pillow until such time as the ghost of Steve Jobs appears to grant you three wishes.

This entire book is about *finding a way*. It's about calming down, making decisions, taking action, and solving problems — or at least not making them worse with freaking out and *in*action.

So get used to it, m'kay? There's more where that came from.

The Three Principles of Dealing With It

At this point, you may be wondering why I don't simply refer you to *Get Your Shit Together*, which lays out **three easy, actionable steps for accomplishing anything: strategize, focus, commit**. *Bada-bing*. And yes, my GYST Theory is simple and effective — but it's primarily concerned with goals you have *time* to strategize about, habits you can focus on *slowly* forming, and commitments you can budget for *well in advance*.

> *Getting your shit together* is **PROACTIVE**. It's an ongoing process.
>
> *Dealing with shit that has already happened* is **REACTIVE**. It's something you have to do in the heat of the moment.

"Dealing with it" could mean anything from having the where-withal to get online and rebook your tickets when you oversleep and miss a flight, or applying pressure to a gushing wound because you stupidly used the wrong tool to cut cheese and you're alone in the apartment while your husband makes a quick run to the deli for ice before your friends arrive for dinner and it would be bad to lose so much blood that you pass out in your kitchen and add a concussion to the mix.

Not that I would know anything about that.

Step 2 of the NoWorries Method requires its own set of skills and tools—busted out in the moment and honed in the blink of an eye—whether they're used to engender a Full Fix or simply to survive.

THE THREE PRINCIPLES OF DEALING WITH IT

TAKE STOCK

Imagine you just landed in enemy territory and you have precious little time to assess the situation before it goes from bad to worse. You're going to have to grit your teeth and gather the facts. Emotional puppies in the crate, logical cats on the prowl.

IDENTIFY YOUR REALISTIC IDEAL OUTCOME (RIO)

When shit happens, an ideal Full Fix may or may not be possible, which means that accepting what you can't control isn't just for calming the fuck down anymore—it's for dealing with it, too! Running full-tilt boogie down a dead-end street literally gets you nowhere, fast. Better to start with a realistic, achievable end goal in mind.

TRIAGE

If the storm is upon you, your probometer has outlived its usefulness, but you can still prioritize based on urgency. Like an ER nurse, the faster you determine which patients are in the direst straits and which have the best chance of survival — i.e., which problems will get worse without your intercession and which stand the best chance of getting solved — the sooner you can minister effectively to each of them.

Now let's go over each of these principles in a bit more detail and accompanied by illustrative anecdotes, as is my wont.

Take stock

I mentioned the idea of "landing in enemy territory" because that's what it feels like every time I find myself in a bad-shit-just-happened situation. Are you familiar with this feeling? **It's equal parts terror and adrenaline** — like, I know I'm down, but perhaps not yet out. My next move is pivotal. If I choose wisely, I may be able to escape clean (i.e., the **Full Fix**); get away injured but intact (i.e., a **Salvage Job**); or at least elude my adversaries long enough to try again tomorrow (i.e., **Basic Survival**).

I felt this feeling when a car I was riding in was hit broadside, deploying its airbags along with an acrid smell that apparently accompanies deployed airbags and which I assumed was an indicator that the vehicle was going to explode with me in it if I didn't get out of there ASAP.

Reader, I got out of there ASAP.

But I've also felt it under circumstances of less immediate, less physical danger — such as when the new boss who had just lured me away from a good, stable job stepped into my five-days-old office to tell me *he'd* been fired, but that he was "sure the CEO had taken that into consideration" when she approved my hire the week before.

The logicats leaped into action. Should I set up a preemptive chat with HR rather than sitting around waiting for a potential axe to fall? Was I entitled to any severance or health insurance if I became a casualty of the outgoing administration? Was it too early to start drinking?*

The ability to assess a situation swiftly and to identify your next best steps is really important in a crisis. Why do you think flight attendants are always yapping about knowing where the emergency exits are? (Anxious fliers: forget I said that.) And as I said in the introduction, you don't have to be born with this skill; you can practice and develop it over time like I did.

HOWEVER: note that I said to swiftly "identify" your next best steps — not necessarily to swiftly *take* them.

Taking immediate action can occasionally be good, such as frantically searching for the "undo send" option in Gmail upon realizing you just directed an off-color joke about your boss, to your boss. But acting without having taken the lay of the land is far more likely to exacerbate your original problem. Like, just because you've

---

* Full disclosure: there was some delayed-onset freaking out on that one, but at least I had already asked and answered the important questions before I started sobbing into my Amstel Light.

parachuted into the villain's compound and don't want to be fed to his pet bobcat for breakfast doesn't mean you should be making any rash moves. (For one thing, bobcats are nocturnal, so I would tread real lightly overnight and make a break for it *at* breakfast.)

Rash moves can get you served up as human hash browns just as easily as if you had succumbed to Ostrich Mode. And if that last sentence doesn't get me a Pulitzer nomination, then I don't know what will.

Just make a simple, immediate *assessment* of the situation. Nuts and bolts. Pros and cons. Taking stock not only helps calm you down (What's the Flipside to anxiety? Focus!); it gives you a rough blueprint for dealing with it, when the time is right.

What-iffing for good instead of evil

If you're adept at imagining the worst before it even happens, you can apply that same obsessive creativity to dealing with it when it does! For example, say your backpack gets stolen from the sidelines while you're playing a heated cornhole tournament in the park. You're already programmed to take a mental inventory of what was in it and visualize the consequences of being without those items. **Credit cards:** What if the thief is headed straight for a shopping spree at Best Buy? **Medication:** What if you're stuck without your inhaler or your birth control pills indefinitely?? **Eight tubes of cherry ChapStick:** What if your lips get dry while you're on the phone with Customer Service trying to cancel your Mastercard??? **Library book:**

What if you have to pay a fine for losing the new John Grisham *and* you don't get to find out what happens????

Go ahead and survey the damage. But then make a plan for dealing with it efficiently and effectively. (Pro tip: canceling cards and requesting an emergency refill from your doctor should take precedence over lip care, library fees, and legal thrillers.)

Identify your realistic ideal outcome (RIO)

WHAT'S REALISTIC?

Looking again at the backpack scenario, if the thief is apprehended ten minutes away with all of your stuff intact and unpawned — what ho, it's a Full Fix!

But assuming that isn't the case, then dealing with it will be annoying, but probably a pretty decent Salvage Job. Most of your crap can be replaced, and it was time to dump that loose Blueberry Bliss LUNA Bar anyway. It was getting hard to tell if those were blueberries or ants.

On the other hand, if you were to, say, drop Great-Grandpa Eugene's antique watch overboard in the middle of the Pacific, a Full Fix would definitely be off the table. Obviously you could buy a new watch, but you can't bring your father's grandfather back from the dead to break it in for you for sixty years before you start wearing it. All you can hope for is a swift and substantial insurance claim — filling out the paperwork for which is the best and only thing you can do to ensure the manifestation of your RIO on this particular Salvage Job.

WHAT'S IDEAL?

Every shitstorm harbors a range of realistic outcomes, and what makes any one of them an *ideal* outcome depends on the preferences of the person afflicted.

For example, if you just discovered your fiancée's very active online dating profile a month before your wedding, there are plenty of realistic outcomes. You may be ready to call the whole thing off, or you may decide to kiss and make up (and personally delete her Tinder account). You'll take stock of the situation by confronting her (or not), believing her (or not), and deciding whether you're through with her (or not), and then proceed to solve for X.

Or for "your ex," as the case may be. Whatever is ideal, for YOU.

HOW DO I FIGURE IT OUT?

The key to determining your RIO is to be honest with yourself. Honest about what's possible and what you want, honest about what you're capable of doing to get there, and honest about what's out of your control.

Think of it like buying a pair of shoes. When you try them on, no matter how much you like them, if they don't fit, they don't fit. Do not go to the cash register. Do not drop $200 on a pair of sweet-but-uncomfortable kicks. You cannot will your size 10s to shrink overnight, and if the shoes pinch your feet now, imagine how your poor toes are going to feel after you walk around in them all day tomorrow. You'll be blistered and bleeding, relegating your expensive mistakes to the bottom of your IKEA MACK-APÄR cupboard as soon as you hobble in the door.

Dealing with it becomes exponentially more difficult if you're chasing improbable outcomes and handicapping yourself with subpar tools.

Be realistic. Be honest with yourself. And be ready to walk away. Comfortably.

Triage

Prioritizing is at the core of all the advice I give — for determining what you give a fuck about, for getting your shit together, and for calming the fuck down.

Dealing with it is more of the same. **Triage is just a fancy word for prioritizing.** I like to mix it up every once in a while and create a sense of DRAMA for my readers.

You've probably heard them talk about triaging on *Grey's Anatomy*. And like an emergency room only has so many beds to go around and its staff so many hands with which to compress chests, dispense morphine, and change bedpans — **you only have so many resources to devote to your personal emergencies**. You need to learn to do *mental triage* so you'll be prepared to deal when a total shitstorm blows through the swinging doors of your mental ER with little or no warning.

I gave you a taste with the Case of the Stolen Backpack, but let's look at a few different shitstorms in action, and practice prioritizing in terms of "dealing with it."

- **On your way to your best friend's surprise thirtieth-birthday party in Boston, your flight gets canceled.**

TAKE STOCK

What time is it now, what time do the festivities begin, and are there any other flights (or perhaps trains, buses, or nonthreatening guys named Ben who are headed in that direction) that could get you there?

RIO

Depending on the answers to the above, you may still realistically be able to land in time for dinner, or at least for after-hours club-hopping — and you may want to try. Or if booking a substitute flight means missing the party completely and showing up just as your pals are stumbling home from Whisky Saigon at 5:00 a.m. (and about five hours before they decide to bail on the planned postbirthday brunch), you may decide to cut your losses. It's up to you, boo. What's your ideal outcome?

TRIAGE

Your priorities should be set in service to your RIO. It's a matter of time and money if you can find and afford another flight out, or energy and money if you decide that instead of making a personal appearance, you'll be calling the club and putting the $ from your canceled ticket toward bottle service for your besties and a cab back to your own bed. Either way, the clock is ticking, which is why we prioritize — once more, with feeling — BASED ON URGENCY.

(Or you could decide your most realistic ideal outcome is to find another flight to Boston but *pretend* that you couldn't, taking in a game at Fenway while your friends are busy regretting their life choices. Go Sox!)

- **Grades are in. You're failing.**

TAKE STOCK

What does this mean? Are we talking one exam or an entire course? High school or traffic school? Did you lose your scholarship or just a little respect from your professor?

For the sake of this example, let's say you have not yet failed an entire class in oh, how about Science A-35: Matter in the Universe, but as you approach the midterm, you're well on your way.*

---

* 1998 was a tough year for me, okay?

RIO

An *ideal* outcome would be that you improve both your study habits and your capacity for comprehending "science" and ace every assignment from here on out to bring your grade to the minimum passing level. Alas, that is not *realistic*. Your best bet is probably to cut your losses and drop the class before it drops you down a point on your GPA.

TRIAGE

Alright, Einstein, time is of the essence. University rules say that any grade achieved after the midterm stands on your permanent record, so you need to get that course-droppin' paperwork submitted ASAP. Then consult the master class schedule and see where you can fit this bitch of a required science credit in next semester — and which easier, more palatable elective you'll have to sacrifice in its place. Sorry, English 110FF: Medieval Fanfiction, I hardly knew ye.

Is it distressing to discover that you are failing at something at which you need to succeed in order to get a diploma, a driver's license, or an A grade from the city health inspector? Yes, it is. Are there plenty of logical, rational ways to deal with it? Yes, there are.

- **A big, bad storm blows through town.**

TAKE STOCK

Walk around your home (and property, if you have it), assessing the scope of destruction.

RIO

Secure the place from further damage, repair whatever's broken, and don't go bankrupt while doing it.

TRIAGE

Here's a secret top priority—take photos. You're going to need them for your insurance claim, which means they can't wait until you've already started fixing the place up. Then put a stop to any leaks and get rid of standing water and soaked rugs if you can. Mold is some vile shit and you don't want it growing in your hall closet. Any busted doors and windows should be closed off to further rain and opportunistic thieves/raccoons. And if the power looks to be out for a while, empty the contents of your fridge into a cooler to save what food you can. After five hours of wet rug lugging, you'll die for some leftover chicken pot pie.

That's just off the top of my head—obviously there could be much more or much less or much different stuff to deal with in the aftermath of a shitstorm/actual storm of this variety. But no matter what, **you can't do it all FIRST.** At least if you prioritize based on urgency, **you're going to get the *right* things done first.**

For example, you may want to get a tarp over that hole in the roof before you start saving the pot plants you've been hobby-growing in the basement. Just a thought.

Get bent! (a bonus principle)

If *Get Your Shit Together* was about bending life to your will, this book helps you not get broken by it. How? **By being flexible when the situation demands it.**

When shit happens (e.g., sudden monsoon rains, absentee roof guys, early-a.m. spider wrangling), it puts a minor-to-major dent in your plans. And while maintaining a rigid stance in the face of unwelcome developments such as these is good for, say, culling surprise Trump supporters from your Facebook feed, it's not terribly useful otherwise.

You gotta be flexible.

I'm not talking about touching your nose to your hamstring (although that is impressive and the logicats would surely approve). **No, it's not so much contorting like a cat as it is *thinking* like one.**

As an example, when my Gladys discovers that the terrace is crowded with humans and therefore feels she cannot eat her dinner in peace and at the stroke of five as she is accustomed, she saunters over to the side of the house and waits for clearance. Grabs a snack lizard to tide her over.

Gladys is no dummy. She's not going to meow "Fuck this shit!" and foolishly strike out for parts unknown just because her schedule got thrown off a little bit. She knows there are other ways to get food (wait for it, hunt for it), and all she has to do is chill (or kill) if she wants to eat. A logicat after my own heart.

Like Gladys, you can't afford to freak out (alienate or abandon your food source) and not accomplish your end goal (eating dinner) just because some shit happened (rude humans changed the rules).

You gotta be flexible. **Regroup. Reimagine. Reattack.**

Unfortunately, flexibility doesn't come naturally to everyone — including me. I'm a literal thinker, which is great for writing and editing books but not so great for adapting when the landscape shifts. For most of my life, if you gave me rules, I would follow them. Rigid was good. I knew what I was dealing with.

But if you *changed* the rules? OH HELL NO. That was bound to trigger a freakout.

How do I move forward? Now I feel like I'm breaking the very rules I so carefully observed and internalized for so long. This doesn't feel right. I can't do this. I'm trapped!

And more specifically:

But-but-but YOU told me to do it one way and now you're telling me to do it another and WHICH WAY IS IT, GARY?!? Clearly my resulting confusion and paralysis are ALL YOUR FAULT.

This doesn't end well for anybody.

Here's a lesson I learned rather too late in my corporate tenure (mea culpa old bosses, coworkers, and assistants), but have since been able to apply in my professional and personal relationships to great effect: **it really doesn't matter why this shit happened or who "changed the rules."**

All that matters is that it happened, they've changed, and you have to be flexible and deal with it. And THAT means being less concerned about *Why?* and more with *Okay, now what?*

Whose fault is it anyway?

Placing blame is a classic impediment to dealing with whatever shit has happened. So much time wasted. So much energy. Why don't you take a unicycle ride across Appalachia while you're at it? Determining once and for all who was at fault doesn't fix your problem, and it won't make you feel better about it, either. How much satisfaction are you really going to get from browbeating your coworker Sven into admitting that he was the one who left the laptop with the presentation slides in the back of the taxi you shared last night? It's 7:00 a.m., your client is expecting a PowerPoint bonanza in two hours, and you and Sven *both* smell like the back room at Juicy Lucy's. Put a pin in the blame game, hit the shower, and send Sven to the Staples in downtown Phoenix for some poster board and a pack of markers.

Remember: when options seem to be closing off all around you, the ability to be flexible opens up new ones. **If you're still bending, you're not broken.***

---

* That's a Sarah Knight original inspirational quote. Slap it on a throw pillow and sell it on Etsy if you're so inclined. You have my blessing.

Incoming!

Listen, I know you're kinda busy reading an awesome book, but your mother, Gwen, just called from the airport. SURPRISE — she'll be here in forty-five minutes, she's staying for a week, and oh, can you order her an Uber-thingy? Thanks, doll.

Can you calm the fuck down? I hope so, because otherwise I've failed you and I will have to "get a real vocation," as a helpful online reviewer recently suggested. (Thank you, Dorothy — your input is valued.) If you're struggling, consult the flowchart on page 154 and meet me back here in five.

No need to panic — this is a solid Salvage Job. You're not getting your afternoon back, but you do have the power to minimize the fallout from Hurricane Gwen. If your home is not exactly camera-ready and you don't give a fuck what your mother thinks about this sort of thing, congrats! "Dealing with it" just got a whole lot easier. But if you *do* care what she thinks about this sort of thing, then you've got a wee window in which to tidy up and a lot of places you might start.

Take stock of them all, identify your **RIO**, and then it's time for some **triage**.

If it were me, the RIO would be to give Gwen a good first impression and then keep her from inspecting anything too closely.

- I'd begin with the guest room/sofa bed. Make sure you have clean sheets or put them in the wash N-O-W so they'll be fresh when it comes time for Gwen to rest her weary, immaculately coiffed head.

- Next, stow all of your stray shoes, sports equipment, broken umbrellas, and half-empty duffel bags from your last vacation that you haven't unpacked yet in a closet or under your bed.

- Wipe down visible surfaces. Leave higher shelves and ledges alone — dragging the step stool all over the joint is just going to aggravate your bad back, and you *really* don't need more aggravation right now. (**Realistic** + **ideal** = **WINNING**)

- Then take out the trash, light a few scented candles, and chill some Pinot Grigio if you have it. Gwen loves that shit, and after two glasses she won't be able to tell the difference between dust bunnies and her grandkids.

Oh, and you may have to cancel or put off a couple of less urgent things you were planning to do this week in favor of tending to your surprise houseguest.

Good thing you're so **flexible.**

It's all in your head

The foregoing example may have been an exercise in physical decluttering — but where did it start? Why, IN YOUR MIND, of course. Recall that the NoWorries Method has its roots in *mental* decluttering.

Step 1: Calm the fuck down. DISCARD unproductive worries.

(Gwen's already here; don't waste freakout funds on stuff you can't control.)

Step 2: Deal with it. ORGANIZE your response.

(Spend your FFs on stuff you *can* control. Like Febrezing the pull-out couch. Maybe there just isn't enough time to do those sheets.)

Lots of shit happens with no warning. Parental sneak attacks, birds pooping from above, or that crack in the sidewalk that caused you to faceplant on the cement and now you're hunting for an emergency dental clinic in the middle of your Haunted Sites tour vacation in Charleston. Damn sidewalk ghosts. They'll get you every time.

Which means that often you'll need to be able to organize

with little or no advance notice: taking stock, deciding on a realistic ideal outcome, triaging the elements, and, sometimes, getting your Gumby on.

And you'll be doing all of this *mentally* before you attempt any of it *physically*.

(No rash moves, remember? That bobcat be hungry.)

In the case of Sudden-Onset Houseguest, you had virtually no time to solve a problem, you had already learned how to not waste it freaking out, and you were able to alter the course of your afternoon, not to mention the rest of your week, to accommodate your new reality.

- All of that was mental decluttering in action.

- All of it was accomplished after you put down the phone but before you ever picked up a dustcloth—by knowing your limits, focusing on what you could control vs. what you couldn't, and prioritizing.

- All of it was the NoWorries Method helping you calm the fuck down and deal with it.

So tell me: are you ready to take it to the next level?
BECAUSE I AM.

Total shitstorms: a catalogue of terror

In my anonymous online survey, I asked **"What's the most recent shit that happened to you?"***

I've fashioned a bunch of those responses into a lightning round of total shitstorms spanning health, finances, family, work, relationships, and more. From bad hair days to broken bones, **I'll offer my quick-and-dirty take on each entry from a logical, rational point of view.**

Now, to be clear — I don't necessarily have personal experience in all of the following situations. (I would never be caught dead wearing a Fitbit, for one.) But if my methods are sound, that shouldn't matter. I should be able to work the steps just like I've been asking you to throughout this whole book.

The idea behind *Calm the Fuck Down* is to **apply universal truths to the whole universe of problems.** Probability. Urgency. Control (or lack thereof). Learning to prioritize. Crating your emotional puppies. Keeping your eye on the Flipside.

And anyway, quick-and-dirty advice aside, in the end none of

---

* I also asked "How did you deal with it?" and given the responses, I'm more confident than ever that you and your family, friends, enemies, neighbors, bosses, coworkers, underlings, significant other, and especially someone's sister-in-law Courtney really need this book. I hope it's working out for you so far.

this is really about me and what I would do. **It's about YOU, and changing your mind-set to change your life.**

YOU take stock of what you see laid out before you.

YOU determine your own realistic ideal outcome.

YOU set your priorities and plans in motion.

I'm just the foulmouthed, commonsense lady who's lighting the way. Let's see what I got.

Relatively painless shit

This is the kind of stuff that puts a kink in or all-out ruins your day, but not so much your week, month, or life. It's not the end of the world, but it's at least mildly annoying. The good news is—there's a lot of potential here for Full Fixes, or for high-level Salvage Jobs. Like I said, I'm easing you in slowly. Think of this section like a warm bath.

In fact, why not run yourself a temperate tub to enjoy while you read? If you don't have a bathtub, a shot of tequila will produce roughly the same effect. Or so I'm told.

- **The restaurant lost my reservation.**

Take stock. Are they offering to seat you at the next available time, and is that time acceptable to you? If so, do you know how to pronounce the words "Might you spot us a round of gin and tonics while we wait?" Good, you're all set. If it's more of a "Sorry, we can't accommodate you at all this evening," then your time, energy, and money are better spent patronizing another establishment, not sticking around this one just to have a word with the manager. (Plus, remember what we talked about earlier — you don't want to wind up an unwitting star in somebody's viral "Customer Does Unspeakable Things with a Breadstick, Gets Banned for Life from Local Olive Garden" YouTube video.)

- **I couldn't fit 10,000 steps into one day.**

Shit happens. You got stuck in an endless series of meetings, you tweaked your hip flexor, or that darn ankle monitor won't let you go more than fifty feet from the house, and walking back and forth two hundred times would really start to chafe the Achilles. If you've heretofore been anally committed to an exercise regimen, this could be a big deal — but in that case, you've also been anally committed to an exercise regimen. Nice work! Maybe your magnificent calves could use a break?

Or, if you've just gotten into this whole "exercise" thing, you may be feeling depressed because you can't seem to establish a routine. Either way, if it bothers you that much, just carry over the negative balance to tomorrow's goal. I won't tell your Fitbit.

- **I got a bad haircut.**

Welcome to my early teens. Lacking either a time machine or an on-call custom wigmaker, your realistic ideal outcome is probably to mask the damage until it grows back. May I introduce you to hats, headbands, bobby pins, barrettes, bandanas, scarves, weaves, and/or the concept of not giving a fuck?

- **My boss yelled at me.**

Did you mess up? If yes, then it's unfortunate that you work for a screamer, but dealing with it should be focused on whatever you can do to ensure that you don't provoke his ire in the future. If you did not deserve it and you're gunning for total vindication, first assess whether your boss is the type of person to change his mind and apologize when calmly presented with evidence of his miscalculations. If you determine that he is not this type of person, then I refer you back to page 115, "Plot your revenge." That'll calm you down and enable you to organize your response — maybe in the form of a complaint to HR, or a letter of resignation. Or just carrying out your revenge plot. Totally worth it.

- **I went trampolining and the next day my body hurt so bad I legit could not move.**

Well, this is a pickle. Much like a soldier who parachutes behind enemy lines, gets tangled in her gear, and breaks a few nonnegotiable bones — it's time for you to draw on the Fourth

Fund and call in reinforcements. In this case, dealing with it means getting someone else to *help you* deal with it, possibly in the form of a burly pal who can carry you to the car and drive you to the chiropractor. On the bright side, you probably got those 10,000 steps in.

- **I sent a work email to more than one hundred people and forgot to use bcc.**

Ladies and gentlemen, forget the inventor of the vuvuzela, we have found the world's biggest asshole! No, I'm sorry, I'm sorry, that was a joke. I'm not being fair. You do at least seem to understand the concept *of* bcc, so I'll give you a pass here. We all make mistakes. There are two paths forward. (1) You could send another email to the same list (bcc'd this time, of course), apologizing and begging people not to reply-all to the original—although in my experience, by this point the seven people in your office who are clueless enough to reply-all will have done so already. (2) You could sit quietly at your desk and think about what you've done. Up to you.

- **I shat my pants (as an adult).**

Ouch. One hopes that as an adult you also have the wherewithal to get cleaned up, dispose of your befouled undergarments, and if necessary, tie a sweater around your waist and head on down to Old Navy for a new pair of khakis. Oh well, at least you didn't fail to bcc more than one hundred people on a work email.

- **The printer isn't working.**

This one — again, straight from the survey — reminds me of my very first day at my very first job as an editorial assistant in New York City. It was 10:30 a.m. and the big scary boss-of-*my*-boss asked me to photocopy something and return the copies to her "before eleven," and it was then that I became acquainted with the Xerox Machine from Hell. It beeped. It jammed. It stapled indiscriminately. It jammed some more. As I was standing in the Xerox room contemplating whether it was better to confess to the Big Boss that I, a recent college graduate, could not operate a copy machine, or to tender my immediate resignation, another assistant took pity on me and showed me where the "better" copier was located.*

5 things you might do accidentally that are still not as bad as failing to bcc more than 100 people on a work email

Ruin the series finale of *House of Cards* before your boyfriend sees it

Bite into a rotten peach

Get drunk and French-kiss your cousin

Make an own goal to lose your team the World Cup final

Run over your neighbor's puppy

---

* To this day I wonder if the Big Boss threw me into the lion's den on purpose. I would not put it past her.

Anyway, what I'm saying is — there's probably another printer you could use. Though I also cosign the actions of the anonymous survey taker whose response to this problem was "on our LAN network, I renamed it 'littlefuckbox.'"

- **I drank too much at the office Christmas party and... well, I don't remember.**

Easy there, Tiger. Crack open an ice-cold Gatorade and listen to me close: *nobody else remembers either.* And if they do, the best way to deal with this is to pretend nothing happened and in doing so, cultivate an air of mystery even more intriguing than your nogged-up karaoke rendition of "Shape of You." Then use the next office shindig as an opportunity to get your nemesis blind drunk and pass the torch.

Tedious Shit

Here we have your mid-to-high-level annoying, unexpected, and unwelcome shit. It's poised to cramp your style for the foreseeable future; it's going to take more time, energy, and/or money to recover from; and the Full Fixes will be fewer and further between. Luckily, if you've conserved a goodly amount of freakout funds — calming the fuck down in a timely, low-impact fashion as per my instructions in part II — you'll be well situated to deal with it.

For now, though, let's see if I can offer inspiration.

- **My car was towed.**

Depending on how soon you need your wheels back, you may have to shuffle a few items on ye olde calendar — and maybe even drain ye olde vacation fund (or max out ye olde credit card) to get it out of hock. So let's survey the landscape here: Where is the car? How soon do you need it back? How much is it going to cost? And in terms of outcome, would you *ideally* prefer to get it back sooner, with greater adverse impact on your schedule, or at a more convenient time, but accumulating additional fines per day? Triage accordingly.

- **I found out that I owe back taxes to the government.**

Without knowing the details of your particular situation, I'm confident that the Three Principles of Dealing With It will apply. Take stock: How much do you owe? By when are you supposed to pay it off? Is that timetable realistic — yes or no? If you have the money now, just write the check and be done with it. It'll hurt, but not as much as a $100,000 fine and up to five years in prison. If you don't have the means with which to settle your debt on a tight deadline, there's always a payment plan. If you're never going to have those means, it may be time to consult a tax lawyer (or Google, if you can't afford a lawyer either) and figure out your best next move. Triage that shit, and stop hemorrhaging late fees.

You snooze, you lose (your car)

I personally know SEVERAL people who have let a manageable debt (a parking ticket, credit card bill, tax lien, etc.) turn into the worst possible outcome simply by avoidance. In some cases the avoidance was due to serious mental health issues, and as I've said, I'm not an authority when it comes to treating an illness that could cause someone to blow up their financial life via inaction. But I *am* an authority on slapping some sense into the rest of you. And I'm not talking about people who avoid paying a bill they cannot afford, either — that's a whole other pooch to screw. I'm talking about people who can afford it but don't recognize that paying said bill *needs to be prioritized* above a half dozen other daily tasks, the putting off of which would not result in losing their car, their good credit score, or their split-level ranch. I consider it my sworn duty to help you prevent such outcomes, and if I have to call you out on your shit to get the job done, then so be it. No fucks given.

Maybe Google Lawyer will reveal an extension you can file for or some kind of aid for which you can apply. All I know is, the longer you wait, the more interest and penalties you'll accrue — and if you think the government is bleeding you dry now, just wait till they pronounce you DOA in federal court.*

---

* You could also say *Fuck it* and move so far off the grid that Uncle Sam couldn't find you with an army-issue Mark V HD Long-Range scope. Good luck! I'm sure that'll be easier than paying your taxes.

- **My girlfriend told me I'm bad in bed.**

You have every right to be hurt, miffed, or purely puzzled, but nothing good will come of indulging those emotional puppies for more than an afternoon's romp. Once you've recovered from what was undoubtedly the Greatest Shock of Your Life and taken stock, you'll find that you have a couple of options—it's up to you to decide which one wears the RIO crown. You could break up with her and await your introduction to a woman more appreciative of your conjugal talents. Or you could take her criticisms to heart and make some changes to your technique.

(Here I feel the need to once more underscore the simplicity that is "dealing with it." In so many problem-solving situations, we are working within a binary—do either this, or that, to begin righting the ship. Pick one and run with it. Or pick one and handcuff yourself to the bed with it. Whatever works, Fabio.)

- **I broke a semi-important bone.**

Clearly the first thing you should do is seek medical treatment, but on your way to the ER (or once the anesthesia wears off), you can spend some time cataloguing the consequences and making/changing your plans according to your projected recovery time. Can you still go to work? What other daily responsibilities may be hampered by your tetchy tibia? Be flexible! For example, my husband does all of our grocery shopping and dinner cooking, so when he broke his collarbone on an ill-advised motorbike outing, we had to make alternate eating arrangements for the next four to six weeks. They're called Eggos; I suggest you look into them.

- **I can't fit into my bridesmaid dress/tuxedo for this wedding I'm in...today.**

Assuming your RIO is to appear as a member of the bridal or groomal party and fête your friends whilst wearing the official wedding frock of their choosing, you may have to resign yourself to looking a bit overstuffed in the photos, then "accidentally" spill some red wine on your duds during dinner and change into that roomy-yet-wedding-appropriate outfit you "totally forgot you had in your trunk!"

- **I failed my driving test.**

Same. The way I dealt with it was to silently curse the trick stop sign, moan about it for a day, then retake the test at the earliest possible opportunity. If you fail again (and again), maybe you should practice more. Or take public transportation. Or commit to making enough money that you can afford a chauffeur for life. #GOALS.

- **The pipes in my house froze and burst.**

As a relatively new homeowner myself, I am continually amazed by the volume of shit that can go wrong in, under, around, and on top of one's house. That any domicile-based fail is happening in the place where you also need to sleep — let alone potentially work and parent — makes it potentially triply frustrating. As such, you might be tempted to waste freakout funds shaking your fists at the sky gods when you realize what went down behind your kitchen walls. But you need to quell that impulse and direct your energies instead to the much more urgent task of finding a good plumber who can show up on short notice.

- **Recently I decided to get a Whopper with cheese at 6:30 a.m. While driving, I dropped my cheeseburger and rear-ended someone at a stoplight.**

Who among us hasn't had the urge to consume processed meat in the wee hours? "Have it your way" indeed, anonymous survey taker. I hope that after you had a good chuckle at the absurdity of your predicament, you swiftly and responsibly checked both cars for damage and, if necessary, contacted the respective insurance companies. I also hope you went back for a replacement Whopper. You'll need your strength to explain to your boss why you're an hour late to work and covered in special sauce.

- **My best friend is pissed at me.**

Is it because you spilled red wine on that bridesmaid dress she so lovingly selected a year ago and in which you now resemble a lilac taffeta sausage? No? Okay, well, whatever the reason is, run a quick assessment of what you may need to apologize for and how soon you can fit that into your busy schedule of reading profane self-help books. If you're in the wrong and your RIO is to remain besties, then get on with it. Or if this incident provides you a convenient path toward dialing back your and Marsha's codependent tendencies, that's fine too. See who blinks first.

- **I've had to go on a severely limited diet due to health issues.**

Remember when I said that everything that's going on in your life sucks exactly as hard as you think it does, and that I'll never be the one to tell you "It's going to be okay" or "Aw, it's not so bad?"

> FUN FACT: In my anonymous survey I asked "Do you hate it when something bad happens and people tell you 'Everything's going to be okay?'" 77.4 percent of respondents answered "Yes, that bugs the shit out of me."

WELL, CONSIDER ME A WOMAN OF MY MOTHER-FUCKING *WORD*.

If you're going down this road, you have my deepest sympathies. And please know that by taking a logical look at the problem I am in no way invalidating your emotional distress. Dietary restrictions are awful and shitty. They rob us of one of the greatest of life's pleasures and are often onerous and expensive to follow through on. Suckage of the highest order.

Calming the fuck down will be challenging, but you do have some fancy new tools now to help you get started. Can you plot revenge on gluten? I don't see why not.

Dealing with it will be a combo of planning ahead and in-the-moment coping when faced with a brunch menu, passed hors d'oeuvres, or a hospital cafeteria. Besides traveling everywhere with appropriate snacks, what do you do? Take stock: What's on offer and what won't aggravate your condition? Realistic ideal outcome: Getting enough to eat and not getting sick. Triage: Depending on your situation, this may be the time to deploy your pocket snacks to ensure you don't get hangry, then seek out a waiter to ask about ingredients and substitutions. Also, for what it's worth, I've heard oat milk is nice.

Really Heavy Shit

Oof. To be honest, I've been dreading this part ever since I started writing *Calm the Fuck Down* — not because it's chock-full of the stuff of nightmares (although, that too), but because I'm apprehensive about claiming to be an authority on dealing with the absolute worst that life has to offer. It's a lot of responsibility for a potty-mouthed anti-guru, and while I have experienced some really heavy shit in my time, I've by no means cornered the market.

The problems I'll be addressing in the last segment of our

lightning round are among the most painful and difficult — if not impossible — for anyone to solve. In most cases I doubt they're even the problems you came to *Calm the Fuck Down* for help with; certainly there are more thorough tomes written by more qualified persons than me on subjects like divorce, disease, and death that you could lay your hands on if you were so inclined.*

As you read this section, you may wonder who the fuck I think I am to tell *you* how to cope with your marriage falling apart or prep for chemotherapy. What right do I have to natter on about the productive aftermath of a home invasion or getting through the emotionally and physically devastating trials of infertility? Not to mention advising you re: nuclear fallout and bedbugs, two things with which I have exactly zero experience. (So far, at least. Thanks Obama!)

You're entitled to wonder these things. As I said, I've wondered them too. But I believe in the power of the NoWorries Method to help you even in your darkest moments, precisely **because it's a different way to look at those dark moments than you may be used to getting from friends and family, or even from your therapist.**

Which is to say that if you find the next few pages of advice brutally pragmatic and emotionless — well, that's kind of the point.

I wrote *Calm the Fuck Down* in service to the notion that nobody else in your life is giving you brutally pragmatic, emotionless advice

---

* There definitely are.

about your anxiety and stress and problems because they're too busy telling you EVERYTHING IS GOING TO BE OKAY and glossing over the nuts and bolts of exactly how to get there.

And much like 77.4 percent of my survey respondents, that bugs the shit out of me.

That said, my suggestions for dealing with your really heavy shit come with the same qualifier I've supplied a few times in this book: **anxiety, panic, depression, and trauma may be candidates for the NoWorries treatment, but they are also NoJoke.** If you are going through any of the stuff I'm about to give a pithy paragraph's worth of advice on dealing with, it would mean a lot to me if you would *also* talk to a professional about what you can do to feel better and move forward, okay?

Thank you in advance for humoring me.

With that, we enter the third and final phase of total shitstorms: a catalogue of terror. If the first of these sections was like easing into a warm bath, this one is more like waking up in a tub full of ice and discovering you're down a kidney.

And although I don't necessarily have all the answers, hopefully I can get you pointed in the right fucking direction.

Meow.

- **I got robbed.**

Whether your pocket was picked, your safe was cracked, or your car was jacked, you're bound to be spooked. And depending on the thieves' haul, you could be a little or a lot inconvenienced. Throw in any grievous bodily harm and we've got a trifecta of shit to deal with—and that's AFTER you've managed to calm the fuck down. But solely in terms of dealing with it—first, secure your personal safety. Call the cops. Think you might be concussed? Call an ambulance.

A friend of mine's house was robbed recently, with his kids in it. He was meant to be performing in a concert that night, but instead he bailed on the gig, got the bashed-in front door boarded up, and stood guard over his family until morning.

Priorities, pals. Priorities.

You can apply the same triage process to getting reimbursed for the things you lost, and replacing the most urgent ones first, if you can afford it and/or your insurance comes through.

You should also start making the rounds of "So *this* happened." By that I mean—tell people what's up, so they can help you out or at least assuage some of your more pressing concerns. For example, if you've got a deadline looming, you'll feel a million-and-two percent better once you inform whomever needs inform-

NOTE: If you meant "I got robbed" in the sense that your Pork Niblets came in first runner-up in the Elks' Club Annual Smoked Meat Challenge, that belongs a few pages back in the catalogue. Next time, may I suggest smoking an actual elk? TV food show judges always give extra points for adherence to theme. Couldn't hurt.

ing that your laptop was stolen and they undoubtedly grant you an extension, because whomever they are is not an asshole.

This is a terrible, awful, no-good, very bad situation — no doubt about it — but neither a prolonged freakout nor a haphazard effort at dealing with it is going to help you salvage your shit. Take stock, identify your ideal outcome, and then pursue it one concentrated, most-urgent step at a time.

- **I'm getting divorced.**

This could be happening *to* you or it could be at your behest, but either way it's probably awful for all concerned. I'm not trying to minimize the emotional turmoil you're going through when I say "One thing you could do is get logical and prioritize."

But, um, maybe give it a shot?

If divorce is in the offing and there's nothing more you can do to stop your marriage from dissolving, now's a good time to focus on what you *can* control and on achieving your realistic ideal outcome. Maybe that RIO is to part ways as amicably as possible. Maybe it's to get the house, the cars, and full custody of the Instant Pot. Maybe it's just to get through the whole process without letting your kids see you cry. It won't be easy, but if you can crate your emotional puppies — for short stretches, even — in service to those concrete goals, at least you'll be "dealing with it" in a more productive way.

Plus: lamb tagine in just thirty-five minutes!

- **We're struggling to have a baby.**

Jesus, I'm sorry. I told you it was about to get dark up in this piece.

I know virtually nothing about pregnancy except that I never want to experience it, which probably makes me the least-qualified guru, anti- or otherwise, to field advice on this topic. In fact, I'm reminded of a conversation I had with a dear friend several years ago, well before I developed the NoWorries Method. She and her husband had been trying and failing to conceive for a long time, and over a plate of Middle Eastern apps I confidently told her "It'll be okay. I'm sure you guys will work it out." (In the spirit of full disclosure, I *may* have even said something along the lines of "You just need to relax.")

In other words, I responded in the EXACT WRONG WAY. The look on her face was part misery, part second-degree murder.

Admittedly, it's possible that I'm about to overcompensate in the other direction, but in for a penny, in for a round of IVF, amirite?* If you're experiencing that same mix of anguish and anger at your circumstances as my friend was, I wonder now — *very respectfully* — if it might help to crate your emuppies for a little while and send the logicats out to do recon.

---

* Yes, I know I'm pushing my luck here. It's part of my charm.

Take a deep breath and take stock: Where are you in terms of your or your partner's child-bearing years? Where are you in the process of trying? Have you done everything you can or are there still stones left unturned? How much more time, energy, and money can you afford to spend?

After confronting these questions, you may not have the answers you *want,* and you will almost surely still be sad and angry — but at least you'll have some clarity about where you stand and what your options are for moving forward.

Clarity is good.

Whatever remains *realistic and ideal* for you is where you can continue to spend time, energy, and money in a productive way — whether it's to keep doing what you're doing, or to look into alternatives. In this way, you're working hard and smart toward reaching your goal of becoming a parent, and you can feel good about that even when you can't help but feel bad about the parts of the process you simply can't control.

If you're dealing with this, I know you've been through the fucking wringer, as have so many of my friends and family. And I know that a rational approach might seem devoid of empathy. But it also might help you to accept where you are and get to where you want to be.

- **France has run out of butter.**

FACT: There was a butter shortage in French supermarkets in late 2017 and I'm not going to say it caused me heart palpitations when I read the headlines but I'm not going to say it didn't, either. Stay vigilant out there, people. If it happens again you'll need to bone up on best hoarding practices *tout de suite*. (And if you think this qualifies as merely "tedious" shit, then you, Monsieur, have never eaten a decent croissant.)

- **A natural disaster just hit.**

I riffed a little on hurricanes earlier in the book, but you've also got your tornados, floods, wildfires, volcanic eruptions, earthquakes, and — the star of my most terrifying nightmares — tsunamis. I hesitate to make generalizations (let alone jokes) about this stuff when my husband's family lived through Hurricane Katrina; my friend's mom lost her home to Harvey; and just the other day, an earthquake 300 miles away rumbled our house, causing the couch I was sitting on to vibrate like a by-the-hour hotel bed — and killing at least fifteen people at its epicenter in Haiti. This shit is fucked up. But if you are lucky enough to wake up the morning after a megacalamity and you still have breath in your lungs, well, you are knee-deep in dealing with it. And before you can hope to achieve a Full Fix or get started on some Salvage Jobs, you'll be starting from a place of Basic Survival. Water, food, shelter. You need 'em, so it's time to find 'em.

But you know that. This is really just me giving voice to your lizard brain, reminding you that your instincts for preserving your personal safety are in and of themselves your best blueprint for "dealing with it."

- **I was diagnosed with [insert something terrible].**

Folks, I've already accepted the reality that come publication, I will be savaged by no small number of readers accusing me of playing fast and loose with tragedy, travesty, and heartbreak. All I can say is, the book isn't called *Feel Better Sweetie, This Too Shall Pass*.

As I have stressed repeatedly, and undoubtedly to my editor's [though not to the legal department's] irritation, I AM NOT A DOCTOR. I'm not an expert in anything, really, unless you count "hating the New York Yankees with a fiery passion." In these very pages I have admitted that anxiety, panic, and ostriching are my own instinctual coping mechanisms and that I often rely on the wonder of prescription pharmaceuticals to calibrate my freakout-prone brain and body.

And yet, also in these very pages, I've tried to show that it's possible to calm the fuck down and deal with things in a more effective, efficient way than by remaining committed to the anxious, sad, angry, avoid-y, flailing processes you and I have both heretofore "enjoyed."

With regard to a major-league health problem, I harbor no illusions that either one of us could just calmly accept something like a chronic or — dear God — potentially fatal illness. But personally, I would try really, really hard to do as much productive, helpful, effective worrying as I could.

Also, who are we kidding? I would ugly-cry, emotionally eat, and request a medical marijuana prescription, stat.

● **Nuclear war just broke out.**

HAHAHAHAHAHA. I know when I'm beat.

● **Bedbugs.**

I've never had bedbugs, but my friends did and their lives became a months-long blur of toxic chemicals, mattress bags, and dry cleaning receipts. Maybe I can get them to do a guest post on my website. Stay tuned.

Meanwhile, I can tell you that we had termites last year and I'm proud to say I bypassed freaking out entirely. Once we discovered their happy little piles of "frass"* collecting in the closet under the stairs, I went into the Deal With It *Zone*, I

---

* The technical term for termite poop. Maybe you'll win a game of Trivial Pursuit with it someday.

tell you. Vacuumed up the leavings, removed all the food and dishes and contaminable shit from the house, called an exterminator to fumigate, then stripped every stitch of treated fabric and had it laundered. Twice. Then, advised by the exterminator to go the extra and deeply annoying step of removing the affected wood entirely—which would require rebuilding said closet under the stairs—said HELL YES GIT 'ER DONE. A week later we were footloose and frass-free.

Those motherfuckers never saw me coming.

- **Death.**

You've probably been wondering when I was going to get to death. Not hamster or cat death, either, but full-blown human-beings-ceasing-to-be. You've been whiling away the hours, waiting for me to walk out into the mother of all shitstorms, wondering how—just exactly *how*—Little Miss Anti-Guru proposes to *calm the fuck down about* and *deal with* D-E-A-T-H.

And maybe I should've stopped short of including this section, to avoid tarnishing what precious authority and goodwill I've earned thus far. But we all have to deal with death eventually—our own or the mortality of our loved ones—and ignoring that would make me either willfully ignorant or a dirty rotten cheater, neither of which I'd want as my epitaph. Additionally, I think about death ALL THE

TIME, so I might as well exploit my own overactive imagination for fun and profit.

To get the full effect, let's back up a bit to Shit That Hasn't Happened Yet and talk about anxiety over the mere *prospect* of death.

For me, this is the Mother of Tarantulas. It's where almost all of my smaller anxieties lead — like, *I just saw the bus driver yawn* easily metastasizes into *what if we die in a highway pileup and my parents have to clean out our house which means my night table drawer which means... uh oh.* Then once I get that far, there's nowhere worse to go. It winds up being a relief to stare this terrifying what-if directly in the kisser so I can defang it with my trusty CTFD toolkit and move on.

Yawning bus drivers? Think about *probability.* This guy drives the 7:00 a.m. route between New York and Maine five days a week. He's entitled to be a little tired, but this is not his first rodeo and he's packing a 20-ounce Americano with sugar, so.

A heavily reported article by a trusted news source that predicts the world will become uninhabitable by 2040? Ask: *Is this something I can control?* I accept what I can't change about this situation (most of it) and turn my focus to what I can (vote for legislators who believe in climate science, reduce my own carbon footprint, move further inland in ten years). I discard. I organize. I calm the fuck down. Again, I'm not going to claim it *always* works; anxiety, panic, and despondence are bad enough—when you add pain and suffering to the mix, you can get overwhelmed fast. But these techniques do work for me *a lot* of the time, and that's way better than *never*.

Someone I know is terminally ill or inching ever closer to simply terminally old? Acknowledge the *inevitability*. This Category 5 is already formed; it's going to be excruciating when I have to face it, so why torture myself when I don't yet? When I'm gripped by the pointy little teeth of these particular emotional puppies, I pry them loose—logically, rationally, and methodically. I bargain with myself. I'll avoid freaking out about this now, and focus on something I *can* control—like picking up the phone and calling my ailing friend or grandmother—before the day comes that I have to take my fine feathered head out of the sand to mourn them. That these mental negotiations actually succeed in tamping down my anxious flare-ups is almost as much of a miracle as someone beating stage-five cancer. I think that alone renders them worthy of your consideration.

But, of course, there's also the kind of death you don't see coming. The sudden, unpredictable, unfathomable news that takes you from anxious worrying to devastating reality: Shit That Has Already Happened. I could try to soften the blow by saying I hope you never have reason to take my advice on this front, but we both know you will, and insincerity is not my forte.

So when that total shitstorm lands, how do you deal with it?

My doctor once told me that a sense of injustice is one of the biggest triggers of anxiety and panic, and I can think of no greater injustice than the death of someone you love, whether anticipated or unexpected. When it happens, you're likely to experience a range of prolonged, chaotic emotions. Sadness, certainly. Even rage. But while depression and anger are among the five stages of grief made famous in Elisabeth Kübler-Ross's seminal book *On Death and Dying,* I will also gently point out that acceptance is the final stage.

And by now, you know a little something about finding your way there. Not necessarily to accepting the outcome itself, but simply accepting the *reality of it,* enabling you to move through it, past it, and on with *your* life.

I've been there — getting the call, crying for hours, stumbling through days, wondering if anything would ever hurt more or if this would ever hurt less — and in those moments, I remind myself that I'll get to acceptance someday because *this is what humans do.* None of us live forever, which means that every day, whether we know it or not, we encounter someone in the process of surviving someone else's death. For me in recent years it's been a friend who lost her brother, a colleague who lost his husband, and each member of my family who lost in one man their partner, father, sibling, uncle, and grandfather. Watching all of them get through their days and move forward with their lives shows me that it's possible to do the same.

It won't be easy and it's going to hurt like all fuck, but it's possible.

And where do you go from there? Apart from grief, which is nearly impossible to control with anything other than the march of time, what are the practicalities of "dealing with" death? Often, we inherit responsibilities such as organizing a funeral, emptying a loved one's house, or executing a will. And morbid though these tasks are, in some ways they can also be helpful. In addressing them, you'll recognize elements of sleight of mind — such as refocusing your foggy brain on detail-oriented plans that require all logicians on deck, or occupying your wringing hands on mindless chores that allow you to zone out for a little while.

At some point, you'll have been practicing calming the fuck down without realizing it. And once you experience the benefit of that a few times, you may even get better at doing it on purpose.

However, and as Kübler-Ross describes it, grieving is a nonlinear process. You may feel better one day and far worse the next. I'm not saying it will be okay. But it will *be*. As the one left behind, you're in charge of what that means for you.

And just remember: anytime you need to let those emotional puppies run free, you've got the keys to the crate. There's no shame in using them.

Woof.

Over to you, Bob

Whoa. That was intense.

But...would you agree that the catalogue of terror becomes a little less scary and a little-to-a-lot more manageable when you confront each entry rationally instead of emotionally, with a pragmatic outlook on outcomes?

And that these techniques can actually be applied across a pretty wide range of what-ifs and worries?

I hope so.

Calm the Fuck Down was always intended to offer you one set of tools for all kinds of problems. I mean, despite my relatively low-impact tropical existence, it's not like I had the time or where-withal to write a book that covers every possible iteration of all the shit that might and/or probably will happen to every single reader, and how to handle it.

But you don't need that book anyway.

What you need is a mental toolkit that you can *apply* to every possible iteration of all the shit that might and/or probably will happen to you.

That, I think I have provided. And in just a moment, it will be time to let you flex your brand-new decision-making, problem-solving skills in a ski-jump finish worthy of our old friend, Italian superhunk Alberto Tomba.

Before you turn the page, though, I just want to say two more things:

1. I have faith in you.

2. Immediately following the next section, there's an epilogue on page 269. Don't forget to check it out for the final word on my own personal quest to calm the fuck down. It involves a feral cat, some coconut oil, and a shitstorm the probometer could never have predicted.

And now, onward to the next…ADVENTURE!

IV

CHOOSE YOUR OWN ADVENTURE:
When shit happens, how will *you* calm the fuck down and deal with it?

Part IV is going to be so much fun! In an effort to put everything I've taught you throughout *Calm the Fuck Down* into practice in one zany, interactive section, I'll present you with a totally plausible shitstorm and YOU get to react to and solve it your own damn self.

Ready?

Good. Because shit just *happened,* yo.

You're traveling far from home. Far enough that you had to fly, and for a duration long enough that you couldn't fit everything into a carry-on and had to check some luggage. Also, you're traveling for an occasion that required you to pack a few specific, very important items *in* your luggage. Now that luggage is lost somewhere between your point of origin and your final destination.

What was in your bag? Well, I want to make sure this whole Choose Your Own Adventure deal works for everyone, so let's say **you're missing one or more of the following:**

- An important article of clothing you are supposed to wear on this trip — such as your Spock ears for the Trekkie convention; a custom T-shirt for your BFF's birthday bonanza (I Showed Up at Rashida's 40th and All I Got Was Perimenopause); a tuxedo for a work trip awards ceremony; or your lucky bowling shoes for the Northeastern Regional League Championships.
- Your favorite pajamas.

- A difficult-to-replace specialty item.

- All of your charging cords and cables. Every single one.

- The framed photo of your cat that you always travel with.
  (What? I would be shocked if not a *single* reader relates to
  this example.)

- A really great sex toy.

How do you react?

Hey, don't look at me. I don't know your life. But for the sake
of this complicated gimmick I'm about to embark on, let's say your
first instinct is to freak out. Pick whichever one of the Four Faces
seems most likely to descend upon you in this time of extreme
duress and shittiness, and then follow it on an illuminating adventure into calming the fuck down and dealing with it. (Or not,
depending on which choices you make.)

Then, just to be thorough, pick another one and see it through.

Actually, you know what? Read 'em all. What the hell else do
you have to do tonight?

Ready, set, FREAK OUT!

If you pick **ANXIOUS**, go to page 214.

If you pick **SAD**, go to page 250.

If you pick **ANGRY**, go to page 255.

If you pick **AVOIDANCE**, go to page 261.

You picked 😬 ANXIOUS

For what it's worth, I'm totally with you on this one. Although I do not know your life, I know *my* life — and if I'd lost every stitch of beachwear I'd brought with me to Bermuda for Spring Break '00, plus the copy of *The Odyssey* I was supposed to be studying for my world lit final, PLUS the Advil bottle full of weed that I forgot I had in my toiletry kit, I would have been seriously anxious. My potential tan and GPA in jeopardy, and, if they *did* locate my bag, the threat of a Bermudian SWAT team banging down my hotel room door — and me without my "calming herbs"? Yikes.

Back to you.

I totally understand why you're feeling anxious. But anxiety is not going to solve the Mystery of the Missing Luggage nor get your Spock ears and Magic Wand™ back in good working order. You need to calm the fuck down.

But how?

We went over this in part II. FOCUS, JIM!

Give anxiety the finger(s): Go to page 215.

Get down with O.P.P. (Other People's Problems): Go to page 216.

Nah, I'm just going to panic. Go to page 217.

You picked "Give anxiety the finger(s)."

As you'll recall, this coping mechanism finds you doing something constructive with your hands to give your brain a rest. Such as:

If you're standing at baggage claim being hypnotized into a panic attack by the rotations of an empty luggage carousel, you need to snap out of it. Why not literally? Try snapping your fingers a hundred times and when you're done, it's time to walk away.

Or, head to the nearest airport tchotchke shop and scope out their wares. If they sell stress balls — huzzah! — you're in business. But if not, buy a container of dental floss. While in the taxi en route to your hotel, unspool the whole thing and then play that Cat's Cradle game until your fingers bleed, minty fresh. There, now you have something different to worry about.

Finally, once you arrive at your hotel and it sinks in that your vibrator may never get out of Denver International — well, there are ways to lull yourself to sleep that don't require batteries. All hands on deck.

Whew. Feeling a little calmer, all things considered? Good, good. Would you like to give that second coping mechanism a whirl as well, or just go straight to dealing with it?

You know what? I think I will try "Getting down with O.P.P. (Other People's Problems)." Why the hell not? Lovely. Go to page 216.

I'm ready to deal with it! Go to page 218.

You elected to "Get down with O.P.P. (Other People's Problems)"

You're having a hard day, pookie. One way to distract from or make yourself feel better about your own problems is to focus on someone else's.

Like the lady with the screaming toddler who was sitting a few rows ahead of you. I bet she *wishes* that human vuvuzela was hanging out in Denver International Lost & Found right about now. Then there's the flight crew, who have the privilege of capping off an eight-hour shift by probing the crevices between every cushion on this two-hundred-seat airplane looking for crumbs, loose pretzels, and lost pacifiers. **BONUS:** If you're getting a taxi to the TrekFest convention hotel, this is the one and only time you may *want* to engage the driver in conversation by asking "Hey, what's the worst thing that happened to you this week? Tell me all about it!" In my experience with loquacious cabbies, your current predicament is likely to seem mild in comparison to tales of greedy landlords, student loan debt, stabby ex-wives, and "that time Eric Trump got a BJ in my backseat."

Feeling a little better? Oh come on—admit it, you temporarily forgot about your lost luggage as you pictured that poor cabdriver catching sight of Eric's O-face in the rearview mirror. That was all you needed—distraction with a side of schadenfreude. But if you want to go back and try giving anxiety the finger(s), feel free.

That was helpful, but I want to see what else you got. Go to page 215.

I'm ready to deal with it! Go to page 218.

Uh-oh, you decided to PANIC!

You're hyperventilating so hard you can barely explain to the desk agent why it is TERRIBLY URGENT that Delta retrieves your suitcase AS SOON AS POSSIBLE because you will NEVER BE ABLE TO GET A NEW PAIR OF CUSTOM-FIT SPOCK EARS DELIVERED IN TIME TO EMCEE TOMORROW'S BATTLE OF THE BANDS: "THE SEARCH FOR ROCK."

Friend, you are boldly going nowhere with this shit. Or as Spock himself might put it, "Your illogic and foolish emotions are a constant irritant." Are you absolutely sure you don't want to see what's happening over on the Flipside?

YES, YES I WOULD LIKE TO TRY GIVING ANXIETY THE FINGER(S), PLEASE. Good choice. Go to page 215.

I have erred. Please redirect me to "Getting down with O.P.P." In retrospect, that seems much more prudent than the course I have thus far taken. Go to page 216.

Fuck it. I've already wasted too much time. Take me straight to dealing with it. Go to page 226. (But don't say I didn't warn you...)

Dealing with it after you've calmed the fuck down (from ANXIETY)

My, how well you're holding up in this time of crisis! You're a beacon of hope and light to us all. You recognized the creeping Freakout Face and you resisted. You returned your heart rate to normal and staved off a full-blown panic attack, so now you can focus on solving (or at least mitigating) your problem in time to enjoy the rest of your trip. You've been looking forward to TrekFest for an entire year — now's the time to be *enterprising* in your efforts to deal with this shit.

TAKE STOCK:

You already know what you're missing. Now think about where you are and how easy/difficult it might be to shop for or order replacement gear, in whatever time you have to get that done. Ruminate, too, on your other resources. How much energy do you really want to expend running around an unfamiliar city all night when it's *possible* your bags will arrive on the early flight into Kansas City tomorrow? And how likely are you to find Spock ears on short notice? Furthermore, if you already tested the limits of your Amex card on the Fest tickets, you may not have a lot of spare cash (or credit) to replace all your AWOL electronics in one go. Survey the damage, assess the recovery potential, and then make some game-time decisions. You got this.

WHAT'S YOUR REALISTIC IDEAL OUTCOME? PICK ONE:

RIO #1: Assuming your bags won't show up of their own volition, you want to make as many inquiries as you can, then get a good night's sleep and muster the will to carry on in the morning. Go to page 233.

RIO #2: The specialty items must be replaced ASAP; your whole trip is meaningless without them. Go to page 241.

Dealing with it after you've calmed the fuck down (from SADNESS)

My, how well you're holding up in this time of crisis! You're a beacon of hope and light to us all. You recognized the creeping Freakout Face and you resisted. You dried your tears, practiced some emergency self-care, and now you can focus on dealing with this shit and solving (or at least mitigating) your problem in time to enjoy the rest of your trip.

TAKE STOCK:

You already know what you're missing. Now think about where you are and how easy/difficult it might be to shop for or order replacement gear, in whatever time you have to get that done. Ruminate, too, on your other resources. How much energy do you really want to expend running around an unfamiliar town all night when it's *possible* your bags will arrive on the early flight tomorrow? (And if they don't, you're going to need all the energy you have to deal with Rashida when she finds out you lost the custom birthday T-shirt AND her gift.)

Evaluate your gumption levels! And your cash reserves: if you already tested the limits of your Amex card on the plane tickets, you may not have a lot of spare cash (or credit) to replace all your AWOL electronics. Survey the damage, assess the recovery potential, and then make some game-time decisions. You got this.

WHAT'S YOUR REALISTIC IDEAL OUTCOME?
PICK ONE:

RIO #1: Assuming your bags won't show up of their own volition, you want to make as many inquiries as you can, then get a good night's sleep and muster the will to carry on tomorrow. Go to page 235.

RIO #2: The specialty items must be replaced ASAP; your whole trip is meaningless without them. Go to page 243.

Dealing with it after you've calmed the fuck down (from ANGER)

My, how well you're holding up in this time of crisis! You're a beacon of hope and light to us all. You recognized the creeping Freakout Face and you resisted. You channeled your energy into more fruitful, peaceful pursuits, and Mexican Airport Syndrome failed to claim another inmate. Now you can focus on dealing with this shit and solving (or at least mitigating) your problem in time to enjoy the rest of your trip. Though I suppose "enjoy" might be a strong word for it; this is a work conference and the best part about it is going to be the unlimited shrimp cocktail at the awards ceremony.

TAKE STOCK:

You already know what you're missing. Now think about where you are and how easy/difficult it might be to shop for or order replacement gear, in whatever time you have to get that done. Assuming you've landed in a city known to host conventions requiring formalwear, tuxedos probably aren't tough to rent, but ruminate, too, on your other resources. How much energy do you really want to expend running around an unfamiliar town all night when it's *possible* your bags will arrive on the early flight tomorrow? And if you already tested the limits of your corporate Amex this month, you probably shouldn't be using it to replace all your AWOL electronics — unless you're looking forward to a stern email from Helen in HR come Monday. Survey the damage, assess the recovery potential, and then make some game-time decisions. You got this.

WHAT'S YOUR REALISTIC IDEAL OUTCOME?
PICK ONE:

RIO #1: Assuming your bags won't show up of their own volition, you want to make as many inquiries as you can, then get a good night's sleep and muster the will to carry on tomorrow. Go to page 237.

RIO #2: The specialty items must be replaced ASAP; your whole trip is meaningless without them. Go to page 245.

Dealing with it after you've calmed the fuck down (from OSTRICH MODE)

My, how well you're holding up in this time of crisis! You're a beacon of hope and light to us all. You recognized the creeping Freakout Face and you resisted. You cast off your cloak of avoidance and actually managed to make some headway. Perhaps all is not lost (where "all" equals "your luggage"). Now you can focus on dealing with this shit and solving — or at least mitigating — your problem in time to kick the crap out of Reverend Paul from Pittsburgh and his team, the Holy Rollers.

TAKE STOCK:

You already know what you're missing. Now think about where you are and how easy/difficult it might be to shop for or order replacement gear, in whatever time you have to get that done. Ruminate, too, on your other resources. How much energy do you want to spend running around looking for a pair of KR Strikeforce size 11 Titans vs. holding in reserve for the tournament itself? And if you already tested the limits of your Amex card on three nights at the Econo Lodge, you may not have a lot of spare cash (or credit) to replace all your AWOL electronics *and* fancy shoes in one go. Survey the damage, assess the recovery potential, and then make some game-time decisions. You got this.

WHAT'S YOUR REALISTIC IDEAL OUTCOME?
PICK ONE:

RIO #1: Assuming your bags won't show up of their own volition, you want to make as many inquiries as you can, then get a good night's sleep and muster the will to carry on tomorrow. Go to page 239.

RIO #2: The specialty items must be replaced ASAP; your whole trip is meaningless without them. Go to page 247.

Dealing with it when you are FREAKING THE FUCK OUT (with ANXIETY)

This is so much harder than it had to be. Not only have you started to panic, your brain is now cycling through worst-case scenarios like that girl next to you at Flywheel last Sunday who was obviously working out her dating-life aggression on the bike. You're not just overwhelmed, you're OVERTHINKING — and this nemesis will *Klingon* to you for the duration of your trip. Look, I know that was an egregious pun, but you brought it on yourself.

TAKE STOCK:

Oh shit. You can't think clearly about any of this, can you? In fact, you've added a few new line items to the Captain's Log since you first discovered your bags wouldn't be joining you in Kansas City for TrekFest. For one, you posted your woes to the whole Slack group and now Cory from Indianapolis is gunning for your spot as emcee of tomorrow's festivities, and two, you ran down the battery of your phone in doing so, so your lack of charging cords is now just as critical as your lack of silicone ear tips.

WHAT'S YOUR REALISTIC IDEAL OUTCOME?

Before you freaked out, it would have been to call the only friend you have who has the right size ears and *isn't* at this convention using them himself, and beg him to get up and go to the nearest FedEx location to overnight them to you. (Pledging your firstborn Tribble in gratitude, of course.) But

now that you've wasted a bunch of time FFs, Gordon is fast asleep, and—
realistically—the best you can hope for is to buy a new cord, charge your
phone overnight, and manage the fallout on Slack tomorrow while you
prowl KC for Silly Putty and Super Glue.

Go to page 249.

Dealing with it when you are FREAKING THE FUCK OUT (with SADNESS)

This is so much harder than it had to be. Not only did you wear yourself out with all that crying, your makeup is a *shambles* and you're without your toiletry kit. Even if you felt like going out tonight, you look like Robert Smith after a tennis match in hot weather. And of course, that's cause for further wallowing. Why does this shit always happen to YOU? How come Brenda and Traci never lose THEIR luggage??

To top it all off, your phone battery died while you were posting a flurry of vague, sad memes intended to generate concern from your Facebook friends and now you can't even see who commented. God, this is so depressing.

TAKE STOCK:

Ugh. You'll *never* be able to replace the AMAZING birthday gift you had lined up for Rashida on such short notice. (The Je Joue Mio was for her.) At this point all you want to do is lie down on the bed and sleep this ruined weekend away. Except — *oh nooooo* — you just remembered you're in South Beach and your favorite jammies are lost somewhere over the Bermuda Triangle.

WHAT'S YOUR REALISTIC IDEAL OUTCOME?

Before you freaked out, it would have been to get your suitcase back at all costs, or at least squeeze Southwest for a free ticket — and barring that, get shoppin'! But now that you've wasted so many freakout funds sniffling, moaning, and vaguebooking, the best you can hope for is to call in depressed to welcome drinks and hope one of the girls can lend you an outfit for tomorrow. *If* you even feel like getting out of bed tomorrow, that is.

Go to page 254.

Dealing with it when you are FREAKING THE FUCK OUT (with ANGER)

God-fucking-*dammit*. It turns out that asinine comments and rude gestures neither win friends nor influence people at airport security. Thankfully you didn't get arrested, but your blood pressure is soaring, your mind is racing, and you're t-h-i-s-c-l-o-s-e to making a lifelong enemy of the United customer service helpline.

Also, you rage-ate a Big Mac and got yellow mustard all over the only shirt you currently possess. Smooth move, Mr. Hyde.

TAKE STOCK:

This whole situation got a lot more complicated when you decided to give in to your anger. Now you've got time-sensitive shit to deal with, you have to do damage control on that YouTube video, add another dress shirt to your shopping list, AND you can barely see straight, you're so agitated. (You may also want to think about how you're going to explain the video to Helen from HR when you see her at the awards banquet. It has 300,000 views and counting.)

WHAT'S YOUR REALISTIC IDEAL OUTCOME?

Before you wasted all that time, energy, money, and goodwill tarnishing both your shirt and your reputation, your RIO would have been to get to the hotel, plug in at the Business Center, put out a few feelers on the stuff you need to replace, and wind down with some Will Ferrell on Pay-Per-

View. However, realistically the best you can hope for now is to not get fired for conduct unbecoming a regional sales manager, and (if you're even still invited to the banquet) scoring a rental tux that doesn't smell like cheese.

Go to page 260.

Dealing with it when you are FREAKING THE FUCK OUT (via AVOIDANCE)

I'm afraid that the end result of succumbing to Ostrich Mode is that you NEVER, EVER DEAL WITH IT. Sorry, game over. Better luck next time.

However, if you decide to change your mind and take my advice to calm the fuck down *before* you try to deal with shit in the future, I recommend turning to page 262 or 264.

I also recommend reading this book over again, cover to cover, because — and I say this with love — I don't think you were paying attention the first time through.

To choose a different adventure, go back to page 213. Or, skip ahead to the Epilogue on 269.

TrekFest

RIO #1: Assuming your bags won't show up of their own volition, you want to make as many inquiries as you can, then get a good night's sleep and muster the will to carry on in the morning.

TRIAGE AND TACKLE:

The most urgent element is to get through to a human being at the airline — ideally one in each of your departure and arrival cities — to lodge your complaint and ask if there are any other human beings who might be able to track down your bags and find a way to get them to you. It would be much better to be reunited with your custom Spock ears than to have to canvass Kansas City for a new pair.

If your phone battery is low, move "buy a new phone charger" up in the queue. If you're still at the airport, this should be easy. If you didn't manage to calm the fuck down until you were already outta there, that's okay — just ask your taxi driver to reroute to the nearest Target or comparable store and pay them to wait fifteen minutes while you perform a one-person version of *Supermarket Sweep*, grabbing the bare essentials off the shelves.

If you're driving a rental car or got picked up by a friend, this step is even easier. You'll have a bit more time and may be able to replace a few other lost items there too — as much as your energy and money FFs allow.

Plus your hotel probably has complimentary toiletries; for now, get the stuff that's only available in-store.

And if the only nearby shop is a gas station 7-Eleven, give it a shot — the teenage cashier is almost certainly charging their phone behind the counter and might be willing to sell you their cord at a markup. (If they sell Snickers bars, buy yourself a Snickers bar. You need it.)

AND THERE YOU HAVE IT!

Shit happened, but you calmed the fuck down, took stock of the situation, determined your realistic ideal outcome, and triaged the elements — and in doing so, set yourself up for the best-case scenario in this worst-case suitcase debacle. Winner, winner, Kansas City BBQ dinner.

To choose a different adventure, go back to page 213. Or, skip ahead to the Epilogue on 269.

Rashida's Birthday Bash

RIO #1: Assuming your bags won't show up of their own volition, you want to make as many inquiries as you can, then get a good night's sleep and muster the will to carry on tomorrow.

TRIAGE AND TACKLE:

The most urgent element is to get through to a human being at the airline — ideally one in each of your departure and arrival cities — to lodge your complaint and ask if there are any other human beings who might be able to track down your bags and find a way to get them to you. Life will be a LOT easier if Rashida never has to know how close you came to ruining her birthday photo op.

If your phone battery is low, move "buy a new phone charger" up in the queue. If you're still at the airport, this should be easy. If you didn't manage to calm the fuck down until you were already outta there, that's okay — just ask your taxi driver to reroute to the nearest Target or comparable store and pay them to wait fifteen minutes while you perform a one-person version of *Supermarket Sweep*, grabbing the bare essentials off the shelves.

If you're driving a rental car or got picked up by a friend, this step is even easier. You'll have a bit more time and may be able to replace a few other lost items there too — as much as your energy and money FFs allow.

Plus, your hotel probably has complimentary toiletries; for now, get the stuff that's only available in-store.

And if the only nearby shop is a gas station 7-Eleven, give it a shot — the teenage cashier is almost certainly charging their phone behind the counter and might be willing to sell you their cord at a markup. (If they sell Snickers bars, buy yourself a Snickers bar. You need it.)

AND THERE YOU HAVE IT!

Shit happened, but you calmed the fuck down, took stock of the situation, determined your realistic ideal outcome, and triaged the elements — and in doing so, set yourself up for the best-case scenario in this worst-case suitcase debacle. Winner, winner, Cuba libres with dinner.

To choose a different adventure, go back to page 213. Or, skip ahead to the Epilogue on 269.

The Business Trip

RIO #1: Assuming your bags won't show up of their own volition, you want to make as many inquiries as you can, then get a good night's sleep and muster the will to carry on tomorrow.

TRIAGE AND TACKLE:

The most urgent element is to get through to a human being at the airline — ideally in each of your departure and arrival cities — to lodge your complaint and ask if there are any other human beings who might be able to track down your shit and get it delivered to you.

If your phone battery is low, move "buy a new phone charger" up in the queue. If you're still at the airport, this should be easy. If you didn't manage to calm the fuck down until you were already outta there, that's okay — just ask your taxi driver to reroute to the nearest Target or comparable store and pay them to wait fifteen minutes while you perform a one-person version of *Supermarket Sweep,* grabbing the bare essentials off the shelves.

(PSA: Don't forget underwear — if you end up having to wear a rented tux, you have no idea whose crotch has rubbed up inside that thing.)

If you're driving a rental car, this step is even easier. You'll have a bit more time and may be able to replace a few other lost items there too — as much as your energy and money FFs allow. Plus, your hotel probably has complimentary toiletries; for now, get the stuff that's only available in-store.

Finally, use your recharged phone to call your wife and ask her if she knows your jacket size, because you sure don't.

AND THERE YOU HAVE IT!

Shit happened, but you calmed the fuck down, took stock of the situation, determined your realistic ideal outcome, and triaged the elements — and in doing so, set yourself up for the best-case scenario in this worst-case suitcase debacle. Winner, winner, room service dinner.

To choose a different adventure, go back to page 213. Or, skip ahead to the Epilogue on 269.

Northeastern Regionals

RIO #1: Assuming your bags won't show up of their own volition, you want to make as many inquiries as you can, then get a good night's sleep and muster the will to carry on in the morning.

TRIAGE AND TACKLE:

The most urgent element is to get through to a human being at the airline — ideally one in each of your departure and arrival cities — to lodge your complaint and ask if there are any other human beings who might be able to track down your bags and get them to you.

If your phone battery is low, move "buy a new phone charger" up in the queue. If you're still at the airport, this should be easy. If you didn't manage to calm the fuck down until you were already outta there, that's okay — just ask your taxi driver to reroute to the nearest Target or comparable store and pay them to wait fifteen minutes while you perform a one-person version of *Supermarket Sweep,* grabbing the bare essentials off the shelves.

If you're driving a rental car or got picked up by a friend, this step is even easier. You'll have a bit more time and may be able to replace a few other lost items there too — as much as your energy and money FFs allow. I wouldn't count on the Econo Lodge having complimentary toiletries, so don't forget the toothpaste and deodorant.

And, rural though it may be, if this town is hosting the Northeastern Regionals, they probably have a decent bowling shoe store. Google it now and hoof it over there first thing tomorrow. (And make sure you pick up clean socks at Target; you don't need to add athlete's foot to your list of shit to deal with.)

AND THERE YOU HAVE IT!

Shit happened, but you calmed the fuck down, took stock of the situation, determined your realistic ideal outcome, and triaged the elements— and in doing so, set yourself up for the best-case scenario in this worst-case suitcase debacle. Winner, winner, cheesesteak dinner.

To choose a different adventure, go back to page 213.
Or, skip ahead to the Epilogue on 269.

TrekFest

RIO #2: The specialty items must be replaced ASAP; your whole trip is meaningless without them.

TRIAGE AND TACKLE:

You have zero faith in the airline to straighten this out in a timely fashion, so rather than waste precious hours (and battery life) on the horn to Customer Service, you make a list of the most urgent, replaceable items in your suitcase and a plan to acquire them.

For example:

Chargers first — Good luck finding your way around without the official convention app. You'll be drifting through Bartle Hall Convention Center like one of Wesley Crusher's neutrinos.

Spock ears — Your best bet is probably to hop on the TrekFest Slack channel and ask if anyone brought spares (for which you still need internet connectivity, hence a charged phone/laptop).

Febreze — Luckily, you wore your Federation blues on the plane, but they could use a little freshening up before you put them on again tomorrow.

Too bad about your favorite pj's and that cat pic, but you can sleep naked, and now that your phone is charged, you can FaceTime the cat-sitter to say hi to Chairman Meow when you wake up tomorrow. Just keep the sheets pulled up tight; the Chairman doesn't need to see all that.

CONGRATS!

Shit happened, but you calmed the fuck down, took stock of the situation, determined your realistic ideal outcome, and triaged the elements — and in doing so, set yourself up for the best-case scenario in this worst-case suitcase debacle. Live long and prosper.

To choose a different adventure, go back to page 213.
Or, skip ahead to the Epilogue on 269.

Rashida's Birthday Bash

RIO #2: The specialty items must be replaced ASAP; your whole trip is meaningless without them.

TRIAGE AND TACKLE:

You have zero faith in the airline to straighten this out in a timely fashion, so rather than waste precious hours (and battery life) on the horn to Customer Service, you make a list of the most urgent, replaceable items in your suitcase and a plan to acquire them. For example:

Chargers first — This whole debacle basically *exists* to be chronicled on Instagram Stories.

Rashida's birthday gift — You're already going to be in trouble for misplacing your party T-shirt; they're all going to think you made up the whole "lost luggage" story just to get out of wearing it — which, come to think of it... Well, anyway, you CANNOT show up empty-handed. The Je Joue Mio was for her, by the way, so that's one more reason to get your smartphone up and running — you'll need to find the closest sex shop *and* summon a Lyft to get you there.

Next stop: the mall — At a bare minimum, you need a party dress and a pair of shoes; the Uggs you wore on the flight won't cut it. Depending on how much those and the replacement gift run you,

you might try to pick up a cheap bikini and a sundress to get you through the weekend. The hotel will have toiletries, but don't forget to buy sunscreen. Skin care is important.

It's too bad about your pj's; that twenty-four-year-old shirt was the longest, most faithful relationship you've had. Oh well, with your new dress and attitude adjustment, maybe you'll meet another twenty-four-year-old this weekend who can take your mind off it.

CONGRATS!

Shit happened, but you calmed the fuck down, took stock of the situation, determined your realistic ideal outcome, and triaged the elements — and in doing so, set yourself up for the best-case scenario in this worst-case suitcase debacle. Margaritas on me!

To choose a different adventure, go back to page 213.
Or, skip ahead to the Epilogue on 269.

The Business Trip

RIO #2: The specialty items must be replaced ASAP; your whole trip is meaningless without them.

You have zero faith in the airline to straighten this out in a timely fashion, so rather than waste precious hours (and battery life) on the horn to Customer Service, you make a list of the most urgent, replaceable items in your suitcase and a plan to acquire them. For example:

Chargers first — It's not just your phone; your laptop cord was in that suitcase too, and if you don't get up and running soon, your boss will see to it that you get the business end of this business trip.

Specialty item #1 — If you can't find a replacement ugly Lucite statue thingy, what are you going to stare at on Helen's desk during your extremely awkward exit interview?

Specialty item #2 — Assuming you manage to source the award, you're going to have to bring it with you to the black-tie dinner in Ballroom A, for which you need a temporary tuxedo and all the trimmings.

Sadly, the awesome martini-glasses bow tie and olive cuff links you packed are MIA, so you'll have to make do with standard-issue rentals.

On the bright side, this will make it easier to blend into the crowd while you drown your lost-suitcase sorrows in unlimited shrimp cocktail.

CONGRATS!

Shit happened, but you calmed the fuck down, took stock of the situation, determined your realistic ideal outcome, and triaged the elements — and in doing so, set yourself up for the best-case scenario in this worst-case suitcase debacle. Helen from HR would be proud.

To choose a different adventure, go back to page 213. Or, skip ahead to the Epilogue on 269.

Northeastern Regionals

RIO #2: The specialty items must be replaced ASAP; your whole trip is meaningless without them.

TRIAGE AND TACKLE:

You have zero faith in the airline to straighten this out in a timely fashion, so — newly invigorated — and rather than waste precious hours (and battery life) on the horn to Customer Service, you make a list of the most urgent, replaceable items in your suitcase and a plan to acquire them.

For example:

Chargers first — You'll be even more helpless trying to navigate rural Pennsylvania without Google Maps.

Bowling shoes — You're unlikely to find another pair as loyal and lucky as the ones you packed, but it's against league rules to bowl barefoot, and you're not leaving your fate as the Hook Ball King to a set of rentals.

The team mascot — "Strike" the taxidermied rattlesnake joins you at every road tournament, and it was your turn to pack her. (Come to think of it, it's possible your bag has been confiscated by airport authorities for this very reason.) To be honest, you're unlikely to solve this problem — but at least you're no longer trying to pretend it never happened. Strike deserves better than that.

You're still down your favorite pj's, but if you win this weekend, the prize money will more than cover a new set of Dude-inspired sleepwear.

CONGRATS!

Shit happened, but you calmed the fuck down, took stock of the situation, determined your realistic ideal outcome, and triaged the elements — and in doing so, set yourself up for the best-case scenario in this worst-case suitcase debacle. Doesn't it feel good to abide?

To choose a different adventure, go back to page 213.
Or, skip ahead to the Epilogue on 269.

TrekFest

RIO #3: Silly Putty and Super Glue

Neither desperation nor silicone polymers are a good look for anyone. It may be time to admit defeat, cede your emcee duties to Cory from Indianapolis, and focus your dwindling freakout funds on getting a good night's sleep. If nothing else, you want to be well rested for the Holodeck Hoedown on Sunday.

Oh, and if you decide you want to take my advice and calm the fuck down *before* you try to deal with shit next time, please feel free to revert to pages 215 or 216.

As a wise Vulcan once said, change is the essential process of all existence.

To choose a different adventure, go back to page 213.
Or, skip ahead to the Epilogue on 269.

You picked 🙁 SAD

I know, this is a real blow—especially after you just spent two hours watching *Lion* on the plane. People might think you're sobbing at baggage claim because of that final scene, but really it's because tears are your go-to reaction when shit happens. It's cool. We all have our tells; some of them are just more mucusy than others.

So what exactly was in your bag, the loss of which has brought on the waterworks? Among other things, that "I Showed Up at Rashida's 40th and All I Got Was Perimenopause" T-shirt is going to be tough to replace. And your favorite pajamas? I sense another sob session coming on. And I fully support a quick confab with the emotional puppies, but if you have any hope of salvaging this trip (and maybe being reunited with your Samsonite), now you need to crate 'em up and calm the fuck down.

Bu-bu-bu-but h-h-how?

We need to reboot your mood. Choose one of the self-care techniques from pages 112 and 113 and see where it takes you.

Laughter is the best medicine. Go to page 251.

You're in for a treat. Go to page 252.

Nah, I'm just going to wallow. Suit yourself. Go to page 253.

You picked "Laughter is the best medicine."

On the face of it, there is nothing funny about the pickle in which you find yourself—and far be it from me to make light of your situation in an effort to cheer you up—but…might it be just a *teensy* bit amusing to think about the look on the face of the insurance adjuster who has to Google a "Je Joue Mio" in order to approve your claim?

When you realized the baggage carousel was empty, your mind leapt immediately to that Hard Rock Daytona Beach XXL T-shirt you've been sleeping in since 1994. You got a little choked up, sure. But I suggest digging a little deeper, and recalling the story *behind* the shirt? THAT might bring a smile to your face.

Now take a deep breath. Connect to the airport Wi-Fi. Go to You-Tube and search for the following:

"Hey cat. Hey."

"Alan, Alan, Alan."

"Dogs: 1 Nash: 0"

(If none of these do it for you, I give up. You're dead inside.)

Alright, feeling a smidge better? Did you, at the very least, stop crying? Good. Baby steps. Now, would you like to give that other coping mechanism a shot to help you calm down even more—or just go straight to dealing with it?

It probably wouldn't hurt to get yet more calm. Go to page 252.

I feel like I can deal with it now. Go to page 220.

You picked "You're in for a treat."

This would be my go-to as well. I don't know what it is about stress or feeling sad that makes me want to engage in some balls-to-the-wall emotional eating, drinking, and shopping, but there you have it, sports fans—if I'm leaving the airport without my suitcase, I'm ALSO leaving it with three Cinnabons, a novelty shot glass, and the latest *Us Weekly*.

Furthermore, there are worse places to hang out for an hour while the Southwest rep "double-checks the baggage carts" than an airport bar/restaurant that serves alcohol, dessert, and alcoholic dessert. A Baileys-infused Brownie Sundae never hurt nobody. If you're teetotal, or if savory treats are more your bag, I have it on good authority that at any given time an airport contains more Cheddar Cheese Pretzel Combos than you are capable of eating. I smell a challenge!

And think about it this way: on one hand, if your bag doesn't materialize, you'll be the odd woman out at Rashida's birthday party. But on the other hand, you have an excuse to shop for a sexy replacement outfit, and while everyone else is wearing their PERIMENOPAUSE tees, you'll be—as Robin Thicke maintains—"the hottest bitch in this place."

Smiling yet? I hope so. But if you want to get additional self-care on, there's more where this came from—or you can go straight to dealing with it. Your choice.

I am feeling better, but I could still use a laugh. Go to page 251.

I'm ready to deal with it! Go to page 220.

You decided to WALLOW...

Did you hear that? I think it was a sad trombone. This doesn't bode well for your vacation.

You moped through the taxi line, did the "Woe Is Me" dance up to your hotel room, and are considering skipping Rashida's welcome drinks to sit on your bed and cry into the minibar, waiting for Southwest to call. Right now, you're more focused on feeling sorry for yourself than you are on enjoying the girls' weekend you spent good money on (not to mention got waxed for). I'd tell you to snap out of it, but you already sealed your fate when you turned to this page.

Can we all agree that this is no way to fly? Are you *sure* you wouldn't like to see what's happening over on the Flipside?

I know when I'm beat. Gimme some of that "laughter is the best medicine" shit. It's got to be better than this. Word. Go to page 251.

Yes, I would like to try the treats. You won't be sorry. Go to page 252.

Nope, I'm a martyr for the cause. Time to deal with it. Go to page 228.

Rashida's Birthday Bash

RIO #3: Call in depressed to welcome drinks and hope one of the girls can lend you an outfit for tomorrow.

Well, that's just sad. If you were going to let something like lost luggage send you this deep into the doldrums, I'm not sure you ever had a fighting chance. If, someday, you get tired of being so easily brought to tears and wish to instead calm the fuck down *before* you try to deal with shit — and then, you know, actually deal with it — I humbly direct you to pages 251 or 252.

Or — and this is a novel idea! — you might just want to reread the whole book. A little refresher course never hurt anyone.

> To choose a different adventure, go back to page 213.
> Or, skip ahead to the Epilogue on 269.

You picked 😠 ANGRY

Simmer down there, Hulk Hogan. I know you're upset, but ramming your [empty] luggage cart into a wall is not going to win you any points with airport security.

What exactly was in your bag that's worth the scene you're about to cause at the United Help Desk? Are you really getting this worked up over a tuxedo for a work trip awards ceremony? Ah, or is it because you were in charge of transporting Helen from HR's lifetime achievement award to this annual shareholders' meeting and now you need a replacement ugly Lucite statue thingy by 5:00 p.m. Thursday?

Gotcha. This is bullshit. You were literally the first one at the gate for this flight — how the fuck did they lose your *and only your* bag? I don't know. But I do know this: you need to calm the fuck down.

Oh yeah? And how the hell am I supposed to do that?

Well, you have a couple of options, both of which I outlined on pages 114–115 of this very book. Pick one.

Work it out. Go to page 256. (And maybe do some stretches first.)

Plot your revenge. Go to page 257.

Actually, I've been looking for an excuse to punch a wall. Suit yourself. Go to page 259.

You decided to work it out!

Good choice. And although Terminal B at LaGuardia is probably not the *most* opportune place to do a naked cartwheel, there do happen to be endless roomy corridors in which you could hop, skip, or jump your way to calming the fuck down.

Or you could try walking in the wrong direction on one of those people movers. It might get you some dirty looks from your fellow travelers, but at this point, they're lucky they're not getting far worse from you. In addition to physical exertion, this activity requires focus and coordination — two more things that are better employed in service of calming down than they are directed from your fist to the face of the United rep who is wholly blameless but unlucky enough to be on duty tonight.

Now, with the remaining charge left on your phone (why you didn't pack your chargers in your carry-on, I'll never understand, but we'll deal with that later), may I suggest locating the nearest restroom, locking yourself in a stall, and completing a ten-minute meditation app before you continue on with your evening?

You're getting there. The angry juices have exited your body by way of perspiration or deep breathing, and you're feeling pretty calm, all things considered. Did you want to plot some revenge as well, or just go straight to dealing with it?

Ooh, plotting my revenge sounds fun. And so it is. Go to page 257.

Nope, I'm ready to rip off the Band-Aid. Let's deal with it! Go to page 222.

You decided to plot your revenge.

Excellent. <makes Dr. Evil fingers>

You're still well and truly pissed off, but you recognize that getting up in anyone's face — directly, at least — will probably not serve and may actually impede your end goal of getting your stuff back and/or getting out of this airport *not* in handcuffs. So once you do manage to exit LGA without a felony assault charge, in what ways might you direct your vengeance? (Hypothetically, of course.) You can't be sure precisely who mislaid your bag, but that doesn't matter in a hypothetical. Let's say it was the dude at the check-in desk whose brain freeze sent your stuff to Newark instead of New York. You could:

Find out his home address and sign him up for a lifetime subscription to *Girls and Corpses* magazine.*

Or

Have an exact replica of your suitcase delivered to his front door, but instead of your stuff, it's full of glitter. And a remote-controlled wind turbine.

That was fun, wasn't it? Now it's time to have a calm conversation with the gate agent, hand over your details in case they can locate and

---

* http://www.girlsandcorpses.com/

deliver your stuff in time for it to be of any use to you, and get in the taxi line.

Unless — did you want to try "Working it out" as well — just in case it suits you even better? Or shall we go straight to dealing with it?

I'm still a little peeved, to be honest. Let's try to work it out. Go to page 256.

I'm ready to deal with it! Go to page 222.

Uh-oh. You decided to MAKE IT WORSE.

Although you fell short of being thrown in airport jail (barely), you did not conduct yourself in a manner becoming a Platinum Rewards member, that's for sure. You whined, you snarked, you said "You've got to be kidding me" about fifteen times — each progressively louder than the last — and then you demanded to speak to a supervisor. A request to take your grievance up the chain is not in and of itself a terrible idea, but you (and it physically pains me to type this), you preceded that entreaty with the words "Whose friendly skies do I have to fly to get somebody who knows what they're doing around here, Caroline?" and made, um, a *very rude gesture* to the gate agent.

Plus, the nine-year-old kid across the way was taking video. You're going viral in — oh, wait, you already have. Your boss, your wife, and your own nine-year-old kid are going to see exactly what you've been up to since you landed. And Caroline? She's going to "locate" your missing suitcase in the trash room behind the food court MexiJoe's. Good luck getting the cumin smell out of your tux.

Now, are you sure you wouldn't like to see what's up on the Flipside?

YES, YES I SHOULD PROBABLY TRY TO "WORK IT OUT." Go to page 256.

Politely and silently plotting my revenge is a better use of my time and energy. I see that now. Go to page 257.

Fuck it. Take me straight to dealing with it. Okeydokey then. Go to page 230.

The Business Trip

RIO #3: Try to not get fired or smell like cheese.

TRIAGE AND TACKLE:

Remember when life was simpler and you didn't just put your job and reputation on the line for the sake of venting your frustrations at a perfectly nice gate agent named Caroline who was just following Lost Luggage/Angry Customer protocol? Those were the days.

Also: I just saw the YouTube video. It's not looking good for you, bud. You may want to save your pennies on that tux rental—you'll need them to supplement your unemployment benefits.

Next time, if you decide you do want to take my advice and calm the fuck down *before* you try to deal with shit, give page 256 or 257 a shot. (Or maybe just go back to the beginning of the book and start over. Yeah, maybe that.)

To choose a different adventure, go back to page 213. Or, skip ahead to the Epilogue on 269.

You picked  **AVOIDANCE**
(aka Ostrich Mode)

Tempting. Very tempting. If you close your eyes and pretend like this isn't happening, maybe it will resolve itself like these kinds of things ~~often~~ NEVER do. Which is why you've decided your best defense is no offense at all, and that is the hill you're prepared to die on/bury your head in. Okay.

And I know you've already stopped listening, but can we talk for just a sec about what was in your bag? Your chargers and cables, the team mascot you were babysitting, and your lucky bowling shoes for the Northeastern Regional League Championships aren't going to replace themselves, and avoidance is neither going to solve the Mystery of the Missing Luggage nor help you defend your league-leading five-bagger from last year's Semis.

You need to calm the fuck down.

I REFUSE TO ENGAGE WITH ANY OF THIS SHIT. DOES THAT COUNT AS BEING CALM?

We've been over this. Avoidance is still a form of freaking out, and you *are* going to have to deal with all of it at some point. For now, can I at least convince you to choose a better coping mechanism and see where it takes you?

Get alarmed. Go to page 262.

Propose a trade. Go to page 264.

I'll just be over here with my head in the sand. Fine. Be that way. Go to page 266.

You decided to "get alarmed."

Your initial instinct was to treat this debacle like the Republican establishment treated Donald Trump in the 2016 primary — just ignore it and hope it'll go away. And we all know how that turned out. THANKS GUYS. Instead, you need to take *action*. Even if it's just a small step forward, it's better than standing by as a limp-dicked man-child destroys the world. Or, you know, as your lucky bowling shoes get rerouted to Tampa.

You may recall from my tip on page 116 that one surefire way to shock yourself into action is by way of an incessant noise. As such, here are some ideas to get your head out of the sand and back into the game:

Set a deadline. Give yourself, say, twenty minutes to pretend this isn't happening. Set an alarm on your watch or phone and when it goes off, spring into action like one of Pavlov's pooches. Get thee to the Help Desk!

Or, dial up the Econo Lodge right now and request a 7:00 a.m. wakeup call. Quick, before you can think too hard about it. You can spend the intervening hours in blissful ignorance, but when the handset starts squawking, that's your cue to get a move on.

Talk to yourself. Not to be confused with sobbing uncontrollably or screaming at airline employees, a midvolume mantra can do wonders for your mind-set. Resist the urge to retreat inward, and repeat after me (out loud): I CAN DEAL WITH THIS SHIT. I *WILL* DEAL WITH THIS SHIT.

Well, would you look at that? You might have some life in you yet. Did you want to try my "propose a trade" tip too, or just go straight to dealing with it?

You know what? I think I could use a little more motivation. Go to page 264.

I'm totally ready to deal with it! Go to page 224.

You decided to "propose a trade."

I know you, and I know this latest shitstorm isn't the only thing on your must-avoid list these days. So how about we make a deal? If you bite the bullet and march yourself over to the gate agent to start the torturous process of SPEAKING TO ANOTHER HUMAN BEING in hopes of tracking down your bag and getting it delivered to the Econo Lodge in a timely fashion (such that you can avoid having to avoid OTHER EXTREMELY ENERVATING ACTIVITIES like "shopping for new bowling shoes"), then I hereby grant you permission to *continue* avoiding any one of the following:

- Investigating those scratching noises coming from behind the wall in the kitchen.
- Opening that card from your ex. It might not be a birth announcement. (It is definitely a birth announcement.)
- Booking a root canal.
- RSVP'ing to Steve's Chili Cook-off. (Steve's famous recipe is less "chili" and more "hot dog smoothie.")

What say you? Rapping with Delta Customer Service seems practically pleasant in comparison to some of those other tasks, eh? So come on — put one foot in front of the other and let's go see a guy about a suitcase, shall we? (Then maybe when you get back from the Regionals, it'll be time to let Steve down gently while you avoid unpacking said suitcase.)

But I don't want to rush you. Would you like to try "getting alarmed," just to see what that's all about? Or go straight to dealing with it?

If trying another coping mechanism means I get to avoid dealing with it for a little longer, sign me up. Fair enough. Go to page 262.

No, you know what? I am totally ready to deal with it! Go to page 224.

Northeastern Regionals

You decided to do absolutely nothing.

Which is why you find yourself wondering what the heck you're supposed to do in Doylestown, PA, for the next four days if you can't compete in Regionals because you don't really feel like having to go out and buy new bowling shoes (and you certainly don't want to wear *rentals* like some kind of *amateur*), but you also don't have the gumption to rebook your return flight home any earlier.

Actually, you're probably not even wondering any of that... yet. You're the type who waits for the shitstorm to pause directly overhead and deposit its metaphorical deluge before you even think about reaching for a metaphorical umbrella.

Let me tell you how I think this is going to go. (I'm trying really hard not to be judgy, but we've come a long way together and I hate to see you reverting to your ostrichy ways.) I think you're going to fall asleep in this lumpy hotel bed and wake up tomorrow with a dead cell phone and no toothbrush. I *hope* that one of those outcomes compels you to take action and at least cadge a mini-bottle of Scope from the sundries shop in the lobby. If they sell phone chargers, so much the better — you do love the path of least resistance! But this is the Econo Lodge, so don't get your hopes up. If they don't, you're either going to keep avoiding dealing with any part of this shitshow and waste four days eating the best the vending machine has to offer before you can go home and continue pretending like it never happened; OR one of your teammates will notice you haven't been replying to his trash-talking texts, come looking for you, lend you some clean socks, and physically drag you to Barry's House of Bowling-wear. You may be hopeless when it comes to dealing with shit, but you're the Hook Ball King. The team needs you.

No matter how it plays out, you still don't have your luggage back because you totally gave up on that, which means your lucky shoes, your favorite pajamas, and the team mascot (long story) are lost to the same sands of time under which you buried your head for four days. Are you *sure* you wouldn't like to see what's up over on the Flipside?

On second thought, yes. I'm interested in "getting alarmed." Go to page 262.

I'm willing to "propose a trade." Go to page 264.

Gumption levels dangerously low. Better just go straight to dealing with it. Go to page 232.

Epilogue

I'm so pleased to see you made it all the way to the end of *Calm the Fuck Down*. Cheers! And I really hope you had fun choosing your own adventures because that section was a bitch to put together.

I also hope you feel like you're walking away with a host of practical, actionable methods with which to turn yourself into a calmer and more productive version of yourself, when shit happens.

Because it will. *OH, IT WILL*. Shit will happen both predictably and unpredictably, each time with the potential to throw your day, month, or life off course. Such as, for example, when the first draft of your book is due in one week and you break your hand on a cat.

Yes. A *cat*.

In fact, this epilogue was going in a totally different direction until such time as I found myself squatting over Mister Stussy — one of my two feral rescue kitties, affectionately dubbed #trashcatsofavenidaitalia over on Instagram — ready to surprise him with a paper towel soaked in organic coconut oil.

He's very scabby. I'm just trying to help.

Unfortunately, just as I descended with hands outstretched, Mister Stussy spooked. And instead of running away from me like he usually does when I try to medicate him, he launched himself up and backward into my outstretched fingers.

Crunch!

I've been asked many times since that fateful day to explain — in both English and Spanish — the physics of how a cat manages to break a human hand. I'm not sure I fully understand it myself, though I'm told Mercury was in retrograde, which may have been a factor. The closest I can get to describing what happened is that it was like someone had hurled a large, furry brick as hard as they could, at close range and exactly the wrong angle, and scored a direct hit on my fifth metacarpal.

And remember, before I met him, Mister Stussy had long been surviving on garbage and mud puddles. Dude is a bony motherfucker.

I was momentarily stunned by the pain, and then by the deep, visceral knowledge that finishing this book was about to get a whole lot more difficult. The leftmost digits on my thankfully nondominant hand were — and I believe this is the technical term — *fuuuuuuucked.*

Would you like to know how I reacted?

First, I told my husband, "I need to go be upset about this for a little bit." Then I went upstairs and cried, out of both pain and dismay. My emuppies were on struggle mode. Then I started to feel a little anxious on top of it, so I took a shower. Focusing on shampooing and soaping myself without doing further damage to my throbbing hand provided a goodly distraction and by the time I was finished, I was no longer sad/anxious.

I was *angry*.

Yes, for those of you keeping track at home, this is how my "I don't really get angry" streak was broken. By a fucking CAT, to whom I have been nothing but KIND and SOLICITOUS, and who repaid me with ASSAULT AND CATTERY.

For the rest of the night I walked around the house muttering "I am very *angry* with Mister Stussy" like Richard Gere when he was very angry with his father in *Pretty Woman*. I imagined wreaking vengeance upon him — picture the ALS Ice Bucket Challenge, with coconut oil — and that gave me some time and space to remember that Tim Stussert (as I sometimes call him) is just a fucking trash cat who doesn't want coconut oil rubbed into his scabs. It wasn't his fault.

Sigh.

In taking stock of my situation, I realized that in addition to finishing writing this book, I had my husband's boat-based birthday party to sort out; a takeover of the Urban Oufitters Instagram Stories to film; a haircut to schedule *before* I took over the Urban Outfitters Instagram Stories; and then I was supposed to pack for a three-week, three-state trip to the US.

If you started the clock at that sickening *Crunch!,* I needed to do all of it in thirteen days. Hmm.

At this point, I didn't know that my hand was broken. I thought it was a bad sprain and not worth spending untold hours in what passes for an "emergency" room in this town when I had so little time to finish my work. In the immediate aftermath of the cat attack, my ideal and, I believed, still-realistic outcome was to finish the book on schedule so I would have six days left to deal with the rest of my shit.

So I took a bunch of Advil and got back to work.

For the next week, I pounded awkwardly away at the last 5 percent of the manuscript with my right hand (and three fifths of the left) while the affected fingers cuddled in a homemade splint fashioned out of an Ace bandage and two emery boards. The look was sort of Captain Hook meets Keyboard Cat.

Was there an anxious voice in the back of my head saying *What if you* tore *something? What if you regret not getting that looked at right away?* Of course there was. It just lost out to the other total shitstorm on the docket.

(BTW, I'd hate to be seen as promoting cavalier attitudes toward your health, so please rest assured, I am nothing if not a GIANT pussy. If the pain had been unbearable, I would have asked my editor for an extension and gone to get an X-ray. At the time, on a scale of relatively painless to unbearable, I gave it a "tedious.")

I was able to ice, elevate, and type (with Righty), and my husband started picking up my slack on chores. I missed out on a couple fun dinners with friends because the last 5 percent of the writing process was taking five times as long as it was supposed to, and when unwrapped, my pinky finger had a disconcerting tendency to jerk in and out of formation like James Brown live at the Apollo, but overall things seemed…okay.

When I finished the book, I decided a leisurely afternoon at the clinic was in order. That's when I found out it was a break, not a sprain. Score one for Mister Stussy.

The next several weeks were challenging. (You may recall that multistate trip I had to pack for. Blurf.) But along the way, I calmed the fuck down and dealt with it. It's almost as if writing this book for the past six months had been preparing me for this very situation—like some kind of Rhonda Byrne *The Secret* manifestation crap, except I manifested a shitstorm instead of untold riches.

I suppose that's what I get for being an anti-guru.

On the bright side: when the storm hit without warning, I emoted, then crated the puppies and gave anxiety the finger. I plotted revenge against him who had wronged me and in doing so released my aggression in a way that didn't make anything worse. I took stock, I identified my RIO, and I've been triaging ever since.

I don't want to alarm you, but think I might be onto something here.

Remember in the introduction when I said I'd always had a problem "dealing with it" when unexpected shit cropped up? In fact, readers of *Get Your Shit Together* know that the writing of that book ended on a similarly chaotic note — we'd been living nomadically for months and the Airbnb we moved into just when I was ready to make the final push on the manuscript turned out to be more of a Bugbnb. I fully freaked out and I did not calm down even a little bit. (I also drew heavily on the Fourth Fund, both at the Bank of My Husband and of the Friends We Subsequently Moved In With).

Eventually, I got over and through and past it — I know how to get my shit together, after all — but not without wasting an enormous amount of time, energy, money, and goodwill in the process.

Whereas if we fast-forward a couple years, in the wake of a much more damaging (and painful) shitstorm, I seem to have become rather capable of dealing under duress.

Fancy that!

I'm still no Rhonda Byrne, but I do have a little secret for you: I don't spend all this time writing No Fucks Given Guides just for shits and giggles, or to make money, or to improve your life (although these are all sound justifications). I do it because each book, each writing process, and each hour I spend chatting away about my wacky ideas on someone else's podcast provides ME with an opportunity for personal growth.

I'm giving fewer, better fucks than ever, and I'm much happier as a result. In teaching others to get their shit together, I discovered new ways of keeping mine in line. And holy hell, was *You Do You* exactly the book I needed to write to heal myself of a bunch of unhealthy trauma and resentment I didn't even know I'd been carrying around for thirty years.

But I have to say that for me, *Calm the Fuck Down* is going in the annals as the most self-fulfilling titular prophecy of them all. I know how hard it was for me to handle unexpected mayhem just a few years ago, so I also know how remarkable it is to have been able to get this far in training myself to chill the fuck out about it. Yes, a move to the tropics and a massive cultural paradigm shift helped jump-start my education, but I took to it like a feral cat to a pile of trash — and then I wrote a book about it so you can get your own jump start at a much more reasonable and sweet-smelling price point.

So my final hope is this: that if you internalize all of my tips and techniques for changing your mind-set, and implement the lessons I've striven to impart — you'll realize that most of the shit that happens to you (even failing to bcc more than one hundred people on a work email) doesn't have to be as freakout-inducing as it might have seemed before you read this book. And that you can deal with it.

I mean, that's *my* realistic ideal outcome for you, and I'm feeling pretty good about it.

CALM

THE

FUCK

DOWN

AND
DEAL
WITH
IT.

Acknowledgments

As a publishing insider for many years, I know how rare and special it is to work with the same team, book after book after book after book. It means we're all having fun and enjoying the fruits of our collective labor, and that nobody has accepted a better job elsewhere. So I really hope I haven't jinxed that by saying how grateful I am to have been supported by Jennifer Joel at ICM Partners, Michael Szczerban at Little, Brown, and Jane Sturrock at Quercus Books since day one.

Jenn—my hero in heels, my tireless champion, and the calmest of us all. I don't think she even needs this book, but I sure needed her to make it happen. And so she did.

Mike—the original Alvin to my Simon and the Tom to my Foolery. He has tended to these books like a mother hen and made them better with every peck and cluck.

And Jane—effortlessly co-steering the ship from across the Pond. Her enthusiasm for the very first No Fucks Given Guide has carried us close to the million-copy mark in the UK alone, not to mention given me a regular excuse to both say and be "chuffed."

Thanks also to *their* respective comrades-in-arms, including Loni Drucker, Lindsay Samakow, and Nic Vivas at ICM; Ben Allen (production editor and saint), Reagan Arthur, Ira Boudah, Martha Bucci, Sabrina Callahan, Nicky Guerreiro, Lauren Harms, Lauren Hesse, Brandon Kelley, Nel Malikova, Laura Mamelok, Katharine Meyers, Barbara Perris (copyeditor and saint), Jennifer Shaffer, and Craig Young at Little, Brown; and Olivia Allen, Charlotte Fry, Ana McLaughlin, Katie Sadler, and Hannah Winter at Quercus. Also: David Smith, the designer who supplied the UK versions of all the graphics for my new website, is both patient and quick on the draw, two qualities I love in a person; Alana Kelly at Hachette Australia has moved mountains and time zones to get me publicity Down Under; my friends at Hachette Canada have helped us crack the bestseller list book after book; and, finally, thanks to Lisa Cahn from Hachette Audio and Aybar Aydin, Callum Plews, Gavin Skal, and director Patrick Smith at Audiomedia Production.

Of course, the fourth NFGG would never have been possible without all y'all who read installments one, two, and/or three. A bigly thank-you goes out to my readers worldwide, as well as to anyone who's bought a copy for someone else as either a sincere or a passive-aggressive gift. (I'm looking at you, Sir Anthony Hopkins!) And thank you to the dysfunctional families, terrible bosses, fair-weather friends, and schoolyard bullies who built my audience from the ground up. Much appreciated.

Speaking of building from the ground up, I also want to thank my parents, Tom and Sandi Knight. They never once told me to calm the fuck down, even though they probably thought it *frequently.*

Finally, even when the topic is calming down, writing a book is a struggle. The following individuals all did their part to soothe me in my time of need: Pépito, Sir Steven Jay Catsby, Steinbeck, Millay, Baloo, Ferris Mewler, Mittens, Marcello, Benjamin, Steve Nash (Steve), The Matterhorn (Matty), Joni, Edgar, Misko, Hammie, Mushka, Dashiell, Moxie, Gladys, and [begrudgingly] Mister Stussy.

But it must be said that no one, human or feline, did more to help *Calm the Fuck Down* come to fruition than my husband, Judd Harris. Not only did he build my new website — a Herculean undertaking on behalf of a persnickety client — he made my coffee throughout and tended to my broken hand and bruised psyche at the end, and he was there for the nineteen years that preceded the writing of this book, including both the best and the worst stretches that inspired it. He is my favorite.

Index

Page numbers of illustrations appear in italics

About the Author

Sarah Knight's first book, *The Life-Changing Magic of Not Giving a Fuck,* has been published in more than twenty languages, and her TEDx talk, "The Magic of Not Giving a Fuck," has more than four million views. All of the books in her No Fucks Given Guides series have been international bestsellers, including *Get Your Shit Together,* which was on the *New York Times* bestseller list for sixteen weeks. Her writing has also appeared in *Glamour, Harper's Bazaar, Marie Claire, Red, Refinery29,* and elsewhere. After quitting her corporate job to pursue a freelance life, she moved from Brooklyn, New York, to the Dominican Republic, where she currently resides with her husband, two feral rescue cats, and a shitload of lizards.

You can learn more and sign up for her newsletter at nofucks givenguides.com, follow Sarah on Twitter and Instagram @MCSnugz, and follow the books @NoFucksGivenGuides (Facebook and Instagram) and @NoFucksGiven (Twitter).

Also available

Praise for Sarah Knight

"Genius" —*Cosmopolitan*

"Life-affirming" —*Guardian*

"Absolutely blinding. Read it. Do it." —*Daily Mail*